JUMBO BIBLE SUMMER WORD GAMES

JUMBO BIBLE SUMMER WORD GAMES

BARBOUR kidz
A Division of Barbour Publishing

ISBN 978-1-63609-817-3

Published by Barbour Publishing, Inc., 1810 Barbour Drive, Uhrichsville, Ohio 44683, www.barbourbooks.com

Our mission is to inspire the world with the life-changing message of the Bible.

Member of the Evangelical Christian Publishers Association

Printed in the United States of America.

002031 0424 BP

JUMBO BIBLE SUMMER WORD GAMES...

great for bad weather days, long cold nights, or any "I'm bored" moments!

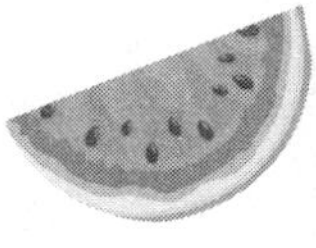

Perfect for kids ages 8 to 12, this book is jam-packed with Bible-based pencil-and-paper games to challenge and amuse, entertain and educate. Inside, you'll find the following types of puzzles:

- ***Crosswords***: Fill in the puzzle grid by answering the "across" and "down" clues. If you need help, verse references are provided.
- ***Word searches***: In the puzzle grid, find and circle the **bolded** search words in the scripture—the words might run forward, backward, up, down, or on the diagonal. If the **search words** are underlined, they will appear together in the puzzle grid.
- ***Decoders***: For every two-digit number in the puzzle, find the correct letter in the decoder grid. The first number refers to the row (the numbers running down the left side of the grid). The second number indicates the column (the numbers running across the top of the grid). After you've determined all the letters and placed them in the

puzzle, they'll spell out an important verse.

- ***Acrostics***: Read the definition in the left-hand column and write the word it describes in the right-hand column. Then place the coded letters from the right-hand column into the puzzle below to spell out a Bible verse.
- ***Spotty Headlines***: Fill in the missing letters of each "headline," which relates to a Bible character, thing, or story. Then unscramble those letters to form a name or word, the subject of the headline.
- ***Scrambles***: Also called "anagrams," these are funny words and phrases that contain the scrambled letters of a Bible word or name. Unscramble the letters to figure out the right answer! (We've given some clues to help you.)
- ***Bible Diamonds***: This new puzzle challenges you to answer the clues by spelling out words in the diamond grid. Start in the center box and then move one square at a time, in any direction, until you find the answer. You may even double back to letters in the diamond! To help you out, we'll provide the first letters of some answers.

These puzzles are based on the well-known King James Version (KJV), the easy-to-read New Life Version (NLV), and the exciting new Barbour Simplified King James Version (SKJV).

- You can find the KJV and NLV online at **www.BibleGateway.com**
- And you can get a free download of the SKJV at **www.SimplifiedKJV.com**

Be sure to ask for your parents' permission and help.

Looking for something fun to do? Sharpen your pencil and tackle *Jumbo Bible Summer Word Games*!

T
E
Y
R
P
A
O
D
A

CLUES

“Rocky” apostle (Matthew 16:18): P ____ ____ ____ ____

Used for traveling (Matthew 20:30 NLV):

____ ____ ____ ____

What God called the light (Genesis 1:5): ____ ____ ____

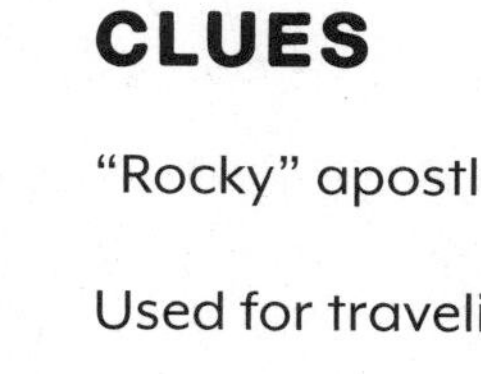

Sweet Freedom

For what the **law** could not do, in that it was **weak** through the **flesh**, **God did** by sending **His own Son** in the **likeness** of **sinful** flesh and for sin: He **condemned** sin in the flesh, that the righteousness of the law might be **fulfilled** in us who **walk** according to the **Spirit**, not according to the flesh. For those who are according to the flesh **think** about the things of the flesh, but those who are according to the Spirit, the **things** of the Spirit.

ROMANS 8:3–5 SKJV

SPOTTY HEADLINE

G●D ●AKES A SEC●●D LIGHT

Hint: This one doesn't rule the day.

____ ____ ____ ____

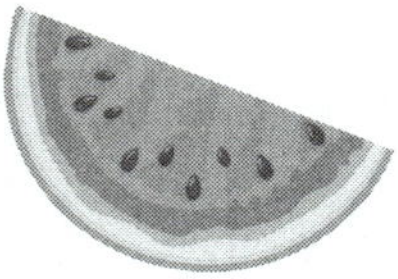

D	S	G	N	I	H	T	R	J	L
H	E	D	O	J	K	J	C	S	I
I	T	L	B	D	Q	T	I	T	K
S	T	T	L	R	D	N	R	A	E
O	I	H	W	I	F	I	E	K	N
W	R	I	A	U	F	W	D	L	E
N	I	N	L	Z	Y	L	H	A	S
S	P	K	D	C	F	X	U	W	S
O	S	F	L	E	S	H	P	F	H
N	D	E	N	M	E	D	N	O	C

Summertime

Across

3. "Then shall the righteous ________ forth as the sun" (Matthew 13:43 KJV)

5. They make summer colorful (Song of Solomon 2:12 KJV)

7. This summer's grape harvest (Micah 7:1 KJV)

Down

1. They fly and eat in summertime (Isaiah 18:6 NLV)

2. Found all over a tree (Luke 21:30 NLV)

4. "Like ________ in summer. . .so honor is not right for a fool" (Proverbs 26:1 NLV)

5. Amos saw a vision of summer ________ (Amos 8:1)

6. "Thou hast ________ summer and winter" (Psalm 74:17 KJV)

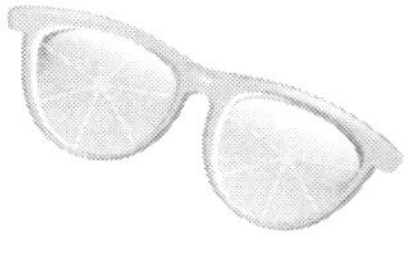

1
2
3
4
5
6
7

SPOTTY HEADLINE

●UGE BO●Y OF W●●●R
PA●T●D BY MO●●S

Hint: A colorful ocean?

___ ___ ___   ___ ___ ___   ___ ___ ___

God's First Creation

Genesis 1:3 NLV

This summer, let's go back to the start. Crack the code to find out the first thing God made.

God created everything from __________ (1:1 NLV)	24-12-1-7-5-9-3
The __________ were divided by an open space (1:6 NLV)	2-20-15-26-22-17
Plants and trees produce __________ (1:11 NLV)	10-19-23-4-27
__________ are found in the air (1:20 NLV)	6-11-21-25-13
Another word for a man (1:27 NLV)	16-14-18-8

15-7-26-9 3-12-25 13-20-5-25, "18-8-15 1-7-26-22-8 6-26

18-11-3-7-1," 14-9-25 1-7-8-21-8 2-14-13 18-5-3-7-15.

	1	2	3	4	5
1	F	Z	S	L	X
2	V	T	O	M	Y
3	B	D	A	J	R
4	I	G	N	H	P
5	K	W	C	U	E

Genesis 8:22 SKJV

"52-44-41-14-55 22-44-55 55-33-35-22-44 35-55-24-33-41-43-13, 13-55-55-32-22-41-24-55 33-43-32 44-33-35-21-55-13-22, 33-43-32 53-23-14-32 33-43-32 44-55-33-22, 33-43-32 13-54-24-24-55-35 33-43-32 52-41-43-22-55-35, 33-43-32 32-33-25 33-43-32 43-41-42-44-22 13-44-33-14-14 43-23-22 53-55-33-13-55."

While The earth remains see

HUGE HARVEST

But when He saw the **multitudes**, He was **moved** with compassion for them, because they were without **hope** and were **scattered**, like **sheep** having no **shepherd**. Then He said to His **disciples**, "The harvest truly is **plentiful**, but the **laborers** are **few**. Therefore pray to the Lord of the harvest, that He will **send** forth laborers into His **harvest**."

MATTHEW 9:37–38 SKJV

SPOTTY HEADLINE

DI●CIPLE C●N'T SEE● TO S●AKE HIS D●UB●S

Hint: He's a nickname for skeptical people.

___ ___ ___ ___ ___ ___

S	E	L	P	I	C	S	I	D	L
P	S	C	A	T	T	E	R	E	D
L	L	H	O	P	E	D	S	C	L
E	S	D	R	M	N	U	H	T	A
N	B	H	N	B	D	T	E	S	B
T	D	F	E	E	F	I	P	E	O
I	M	W	V	E	S	T	H	V	R
F	W	O	W	Y	P	L	E	R	E
U	M	K	V	R	N	U	R	A	R
L	V	X	K	V	M	M	D	H	S

A Time And A Place

Ecclesiastes 3:1 KJV

Each new season reminds us of how beautiful life is. . .and how important it is that we make the most of it. Crack the code to discover the right attitude toward change.

"A time to pluck up that which is _________ " (3:2 KJV) 29-17-2-22-41-25-7

"A time to laugh; a time to _________ " (3:4 KJV) 24-3-35-34-39

"A time to _________ stones together" (3:5 KJV) 8-6-37-4-32-36

"A time to keep _________ and a time to speak" (3:7 SKJV) 30-10-28-20-19-26-42

Hard, discouraging work (3:10 KJV) 23-18-27-9-12-5-38

"He has made _________ beautiful in its time" (3:11) 14-33-16-31-40-1-11-13-15-21

41-3 25-9-32-34-40 37-11-10-39-8 1-4-20-36-32 5-30 2

30-14-27-30-3-15, 27-39-7 12 37-5-24-25 23-3

16-33-20-34-40 29-35-36-29-3-30-25 35-39-7-32-36

41-11-14 11-16-27-33-14-39.

H
A
A
J
L
Y
I
E
F

CLUES

Given in abundance (John 10:10): L ____ ____ ____

Prophet of fire (1 Kings 18:36–37):

____ ____ ____ ____ ____ ____

Easily burnt, like wood and stubble (1 Corinthians 3:12 KJV, SKJV): ____ ____ ____

IN THE GARDEN

Across

3. God covered Adam and Eve with ________ (Genesis 3:21)

6. Name of the garden (Genesis 2:15)

7. "The ________ was more subtil than any beast" (Genesis 3:1 KJV)

10. "The day you eat from it you will ________" (Genesis 2:17 NLV)

Down

1. "They sewed ________ leaves together" (Genesis 3:7 KJV)

2. The fruit was ________ to Eve's eyes (Genesis 3:6 KJV)

4. "You will eat bread by the ________ of your face" (Genesis 3:19 NLV)

5. "He will crush [the serpent's] ________, and [the serpent] will crush his heel" (Genesis 3:15 NLV)

8. God made Eve from Adam's ________ (Genesis 2:22 KJV)

9. "I was afraid, because I was ________" (Genesis 3:10 KJV)

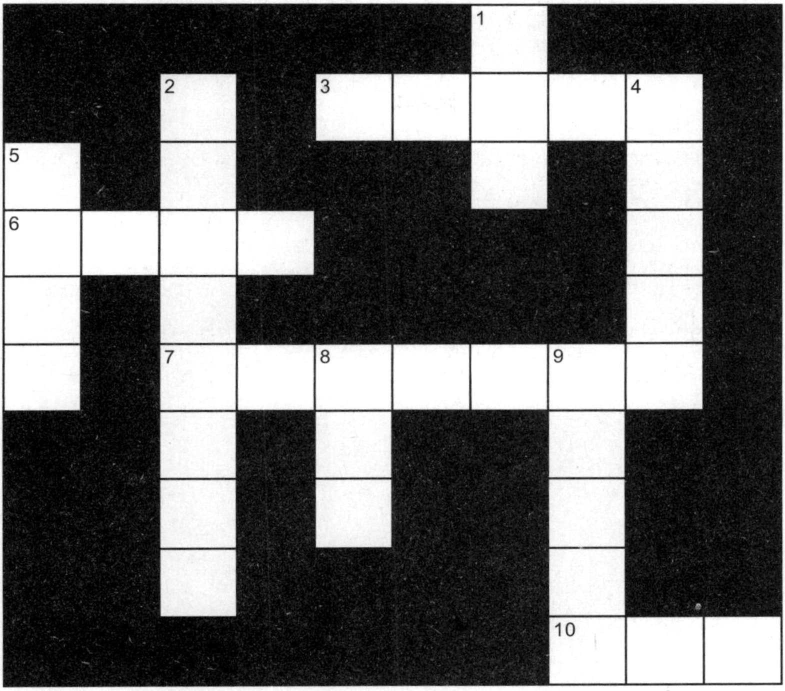
1
2
3
4
5
6
7
8
9
10

SPOTTY HEADLINE

●HE● JESUS M●●ES
● ●AY, PE●E● DOE●
THE IMP●SSIB●●

Hint: The disciple never could have done it without Jesus' help.

STEPHEN'S LAST VISION

When they heard these things, they were **cut** to the **heart**, and they **gnashed** at him with their **teeth**. But he, being full of the **Holy Spirit**, looked up steadfastly into heaven and saw the glory of God, and Jesus **standing** at the **right hand** of God, and said, "**Behold**, I see the heavens **opened** and the Son of Man standing at the right hand of God." Then they **cried** out with a loud voice, and **stopped** their **ears**, and **ran at** him with one **accord**.

ACTS 7:54–57 SKJV

SPOTTY HEADLINE

ISR●E●ITES CONSTRU●T
●A●SE ●O● N●AR M●UNTAI●

Hint: This pricey idol didn't deserve their worship.

___ ___ ___ ___ ___ ___

___ ___ ___ ___

T	N	D	G	N	A	S	H	E	D
A	I	R	E	Z	P	B	G	F	N
N	S	R	B	P	E	A	R	S	A
A	T	J	I	H	P	D	M	V	H
R	A	E	O	P	E	O	A	J	T
T	N	L	E	I	S	C	T	R	H
U	D	W	R	T	C	Y	A	S	G
C	I	C	D	O	H	E	L	H	I
L	N	B	R	Y	H	M	V	O	R
J	G	D	E	N	E	P	O	K	H

WHAT LASTS FOREVER

ISAIAH 40:8 SKJV

Nothing lasts forever. . .except one thing.
Crack the code to find out what that is.

"Make the road in the desert
__________" (40:3 NLV) 13-23-20-33-36-34-42-12

"All __________ is grass" (40:6 KJV, SKJV) 38-21-41-10-4

"__________ your God!" (40:9 KJV, SKJV) 15-44-5-17-1-14

Empty; another word for palm
(40:12 KJV) 11-22-24-43-18-16

Knowledge; wisdom
(40:14) 28-19-31-39-29-9-40-2-3-32-35-7-37

Second to gold (40:19) 27-6-25-30-8-26

23-42-41 34-20-33-13-9 16-6-12-4-44-29-27, 40-42-41

38-21-17-16-8-29 38-33-14-41-10, 15-28-12 12-5-8

16-18-26-32 22-38 17-28-26 34-18-14 27-5-33-21-1

9-12-2-3-14 38-17-20-44-30-8-20.

DECODER

	1	2	3	4	5
1	H	D	P	E	K
2	B	Q	I	A	V
3	G	N	C	W	U
4	R	M	J	F	Y
5	S	T	Z	O	L

John 8:36 KJV

23-44 52-11-14 51-54-32 52-11-14-41-14-44-54-41-14

51-11-24-55-55 42-24-15-14 45-54-35 44-41-14-14, 45-14

51-11-24-55-55 21-14 44-41-14-14 23-32-12-14-14-12.

Love

Across

3. "A ________ loveth at all times" (Proverbs 17:17 KJV)
4. "Love is the fulfilling of the ________" (Romans 13:10 KJV)
6. Another word for "love" in the KJV (1 Corinthians 13)
7. "Let us not love in word. . .but in deed and in ________" (1 John 3:18 KJV)
8. "While we were yet ________, Christ died for us" (Romans 5:8 KJV)

Down

1. "Faith and hope and love, but the ________ of these is love" (1 Corinthians 13:13 NLV)
2. "Perfect love casteth out ________" (1 John 4:18 KJV)
5. "For God so loved the ________. . ." (John 3:16 KJV)
6. "Love ________ all sins" (Proverbs 10:12 NLV)

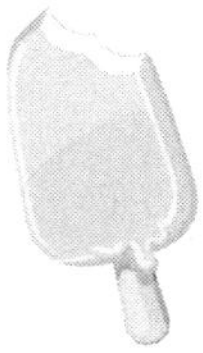

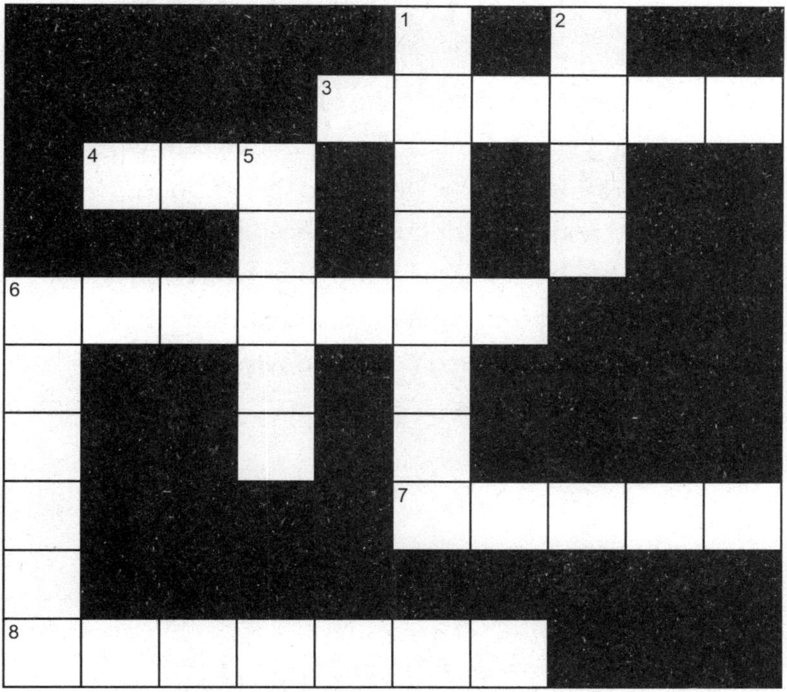
1
2
3
4
5
6
7
8

SCRAMBLED THING

SHADY EVENT

Hint: When God rested

___ ___ ___ ___ ___ ___ ___

___ ___ ___

Colorful Promise

I will set My **rainbow** in the cloud, and it will be something **special** to see because of an **agreement** between Me and the earth. When I bring clouds over the earth and the rainbow **is seen** in the clouds, I will **remember** My agreement that is **between** Me and you and **every** living thing of all flesh. **Never** again will the **water** become a **flood** to **destroy all flesh**.

GENESIS 9:13–15 NLV

SPOTTY HEADLINE

TE● SPIES AFR●ID THEY ●A●'T T●KE THIS L●ND

Hint: It had been promised to them!

___ ___ ___ ___ ___ ___

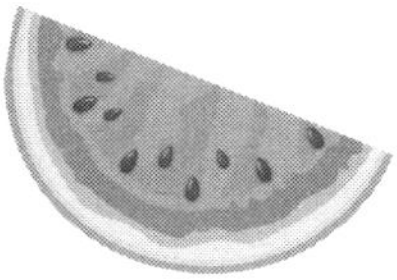

A	Z	R	E	V	E	N	E	L	L
L	I	R	R	K	V	V	D	A	R
L	Y	S	R	E	E	H	I	N	E
F	O	W	S	R	T	C	H	E	M
L	R	O	Y	E	E	A	D	E	E
E	T	B	R	P	E	O	W	W	M
S	S	N	S	Z	O	N	F	T	B
H	E	I	Y	L	P	L	T	E	E
L	D	A	F	B	L	V	M	B	R
A	G	R	E	E	M	E	N	T	R

A
E
R
N
S
T
I
H
N

CLUES

Separates from God (Isaiah 59:2): S ___ ___

How many hundreds of years Adam lived (Genesis 5:5): ___ ___ ___ ___

A new one's coming (Revelation 21:1):

___ ___ ___ ___ ___

A Joyous Season

Song of Solomon 2:12 skjv

In this beautiful song, a couple expresses their love for each other. Crack the code to find out when the song takes place.

"I am the ___ of Sharon" (2:1) 35-25-10-34

Keeps the doctor away (2:3 kjv, skjv) 30-1-13-32-11

"He ___ me to the banqueting house" (2:4 kjv, kjv) 19-40-9-36-29-12-18

"Behold, he ___ leaping on the mountains" (2:8 skjv) 7-23-39-15-31

"Rise up, my love, my ___ one" (2:10 kjv) 4-24-33-8-22-26-20-28-3

"For behold, the ___ is past. The rain is over and gone" (2:11 kjv, skjv) 6-17-21-38-37-2

A graceful bird (2:14) 16-5-14-27

18-12-34 20-3-5-6-37-2-31 33-13-1-11-30-40 25-21

22-12-15 24-30-35-38-12. 18-12-27 22-17-39-15 5-20

38-12-37 10-26-21-29-17-21-29 5-20 19-17-2-16-31 12-30-31

7-5-39-24, 33-21-16 38-12-37 14-5-17-7-27 23-20 22-12-27

18-8-2-38-3-24-16-9-14-37 26-31 12-27-33-2-16 17-21 5-36-2

3-33-21-16.

CROSSWORD

Keep Working!

Across

3. An unbeliever; better off than someone who doesn't work (1 Timothy 5:8 KJV)

5. "Do all to the ________ of God" (1 Corinthians 10:31 KJV)

6. "Go to the ________ , thou sluggard" (Proverbs 6:6 KJV)

8. "The Lord God. . .put [Adam] in the garden of Eden to work the ________" (Genesis 2:15 NLV)

9. "With good ________ doing service" (Ephesians 6:7 KJV)

Down

1. "He who ________ his land shall be satisfied with bread" (Proverbs 12:11 SKJV)

2. "The soul of the ________ desires and has nothing" (Proverbs 13:4 SKJV)

4. Lazy; like a slow creature (Proverbs 18:9 KJV)

7. "Nothing but talk leads only to being ________" (Proverbs 14:23 NLV)

1
2
3
4
5
6
7
8
9

SPOTTY HEADLINE

MAN EN●OYS DREAM
●F ●LIM●ING ●NGELS

Hint: He saw them on a ladder to heaven!

___ ___ ___ ___ ___

WORD SEARCH

STORMY WEATHER

Listen to the **thunder** of His voice and the **noise** that comes from His **mouth**. He lets it loose under the **whole** heaven. He lets His **lightning** go to the ends of the **earth**. His **voice** sounds after it. He thunders with His **great** and **powerful** voice. And He does not **hold back** the lightning when His voice is **heard**.

Job 37:2–4 NLV

SCRAMBLED THING

BASS LOVER PAM

Hint: What the Israelites sacrificed. . . and what Jesus was

___ ___ ___ ___ ___ ___ ___ ___

___ ___ ___ ___

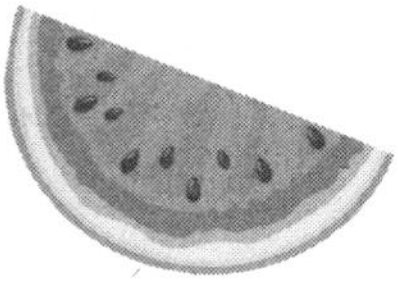

K	C	A	B	D	L	O	H	R	G
N	O	I	S	E	D	E	E	D	N
N	Z	M	K	M	A	D	R	P	I
E	G	Y	O	R	N	A	G	D	N
T	M	T	T	U	E	K	R	F	T
S	W	H	H	H	T	W	E	N	H
I	H	T	K	N	K	H	A	H	G
L	O	C	P	J	N	W	T	X	I
F	L	V	R	E	C	I	O	V	L
R	E	P	O	W	E	R	F	U	L

FORBIDDEN TREAT

1 SAMUEL 14:25 SKJV

Saul's son, Jonathan, found a delicious food on the ground. . .but eating it almost cost him his life. Crack the code to find out what it was.

"_________ is the man who eats any food until evening" (14:24 SKJV) 4-3-13-5-6-23

". . .that I may take _________ on my enemies" (14:24 SKJV) 15-22-33-27-12-16-32-7-1

"No man put his hand to his _________" (14:26 KJV, SKJV) 17-18-21-14-30

Without limitation or hesitation (14:30 KJV, SKJV) 9-2-24-11-26-19

"Shall Jonathan die, who hath _________ this great salvation in Israel?" (14:45 KJV) 25-31-28-29-10-20-8

16-33-23 16-26-26 8-30-28-5-22 18-9 14-20-6

26-16-32-23 7-16-17-24 8-28 16 25-18-28-23,

16-33-23 14-30-11-2-1 25-16-5 20-18-33-24-19 28-32

14-20-6 10-31-18-29-33-23.

DECODER

	1	2	3	4	5
1	R	B	X	W	H
2	M	P	G	L	V
3	S	A	C	Z	O
4	F	N	Y	K	T
5	D	E	I	U	J

Psalm 93:4 KJV

45-15-52 24-35-11-51 35-42 15-53-23-15 53-31

21-53-23-15-45-53-52-11 45-15-32-42 45-15-52

42-35-53-31-52 35-41 21-32-42-43 14-32-45-52-11-31,

43-52-32, 45-15-32-42 45-15-52 21-53-23-15-45-43

14-32-25-52-31 35-41 45-15-52 31-52-32.

DON'T WORRY!

MATTHEW 6:29 KJV

When telling us not to worry, Jesus used the carefree lilies as an example. Crack the code to find out what He had to say about them.

"[The birds] do not _________ grain" (6:26 NLV) 20-1-28-13-27-17

What lilies are (6:29 NLV) 30-3-26-32-10-15-8

Used for burning grass (6:30 KJV, SKJV) 16-12-19-11

"What shall we eat? or, What shall we _________?" (6:31 KJV) 21-9-31-23-14

"Look for the _________ nation of God" (6:33 NLV) 24-2-18-34

"Don't worry about _________" (6:34 SKJV) 4-22-33-5-6-7-29-25

Where you should put God's kingdom 35-38-37-39-36

27-12-15-23 10-16-18-22-33-16-11 31-23 1-18-18 13-31-32

20-18-2-7-34 25-1-10 11-29-28 1-17-6-1-34-27-21 18-31-14-19

5-11-27 16-35 4-24-27-39-19.

N
T
U
R
S
N
I
O
L

CLUES

Not as bright as God's glory (Revelation 21:23): S ____ ____

Joshua's dad (Exodus 33:11): ____ ____ ____

Part of your nose (Genesis 2:7 KJV, SKJV): ____ ____ ____ ____ ____ ____ ____

WORD SEARCH

SHADE AND SHELTER

For You have been a **strength** to the poor, a strength to the **needy** in his **distress**, a **refuge** from the **storm**, a **shadow** from the heat, when the **blast** of the **terrifying** ones is as a storm against the wall. You shall bring **down** the noise of foreigners, as the heat in a **dry place**, the heat with the shadow of a **cloud**. The **branch** of the terrifying ones shall be brought **low**.

Isaiah 25:4–5 SKJV

SPOTTY HEADLINE

●OM●TH●NG OCCU●S TO JE●US' BODY

Hint: He got up from the dead!

___ ___ ___ ___ ___

D	I	S	T	R	E	S	S	Y	W
E	L	H	H	C	N	A	R	B	D
C	S	T	S	A	L	B	Y	U	V
A	T	G	W	F	Y	D	O	K	S
L	O	N	R	M	E	L	V	H	N
P	R	E	N	E	C	B	A	M	Q
Y	M	R	N	W	F	D	L	M	M
R	N	T	Q	M	O	U	N	O	H
D	J	S	R	W	C	D	G	F	W
G	N	I	Y	F	I	R	R	E	T

FAITH

Across

1. "Your faith should not stand in the _________ of men" (1 Corinthians 2:5 KJV)

4. "Without faith it is _________ to please" God (Hebrews 11:6 KJV)

6. "For by _________ are ye saved through faith" (Ephesians 2:8 KJV)

7. "The _________ shall live by faith" (Romans 1:17 KJV)

Down

1. "Go thy way; thy faith hath made thee _________" (Mark 10:52 KJV)

2. "I have fought a good _________ . . .I have kept the faith" (2 Timothy 4:7 KJV)

3. "If thou shalt. . .believe in thine _________" (Romans 10:9 KJV)

5. "And the apostles said unto the Lord, _________ our faith" (Luke 17:5 KJV)

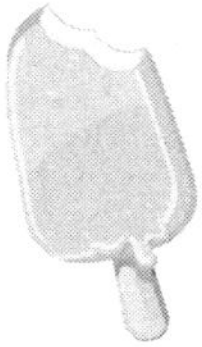

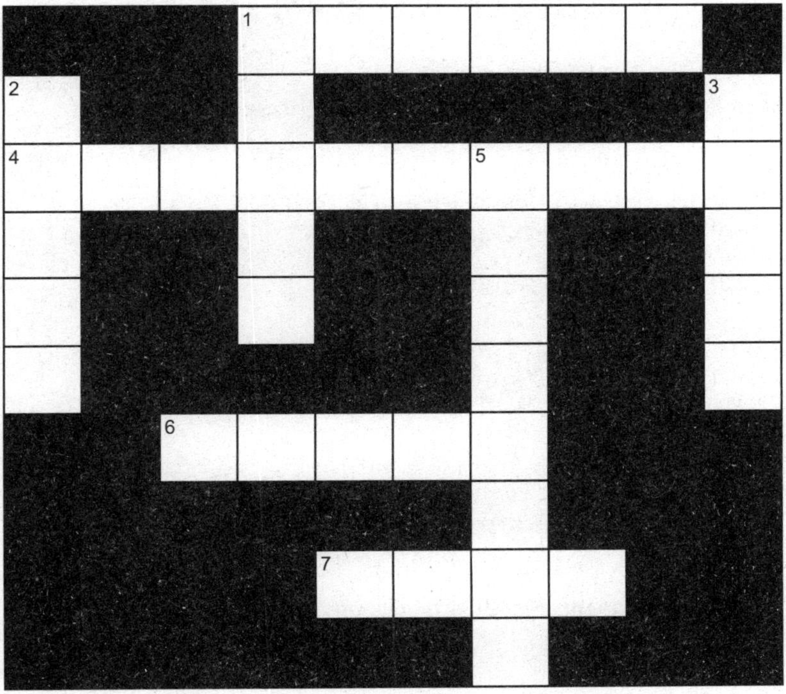
1
2
3
4
5
6
7

SPOTTY HEADLINE

E●Y●T ST●NNED BY T●N C●●AMITIE●

Hint: Moses sent them on Pharaoh.

___ ___ ___ ___ ___ ___ ___

HALL OF FAITH

HEBREWS 11:1 KJV

God loves it when His children have faith. Crack the code to find out what faith truly is.

"By faith ________ was taken up that he should not see death" (11:5 SKJV) 2-46-13-42-43

Noah "became heir of the ________ which is by faith" (11:7 KJV) 3-9-22-35-23-26-37-33-28-11-15-16-41

"For [Abraham] looked for a city which hath ________" (11:10 KJV) 38-10-12-24-39-5-27-14-18-45-47

Moses was hidden three months after he was ________ (11:23) 4-44-31-6

Through faith Moses kept the ________ (11:28) 34-8-7-1-19-20-21-25

Fate of the Egyptians in the Red Sea (11:29 KJV, SKJV) 32-36-48-17-30-40-29

46-13-17 38-5-9-23-43 14-16 27-35-26

41-12-4-28-23-8-6-42-2 10-38 23-43-14-30-22-7

43-19-34-2-39 38-48-3, 27-35-2 21-20-9-39-40-46-42-21

10-38 23-43-9-46-22-1 11-19-27 7-2-21-30.

DECODER

	1	2	3	4	5
1	F	Z	I	Y	K
2	X	W	N	L	S
3	D	C	V	P	E
4	M	J	B	G	A
5	H	T	U	R	O

Luke 12:55 SKJV

45-23-31 22-51-35-23 14-55-53 25-35-35 52-51-35

25-55-53-52-51 22-13-23-31 43-24-55-22, 14-55-53

25-45-14, “52-51-35-54-35 22-13-24-24 43-35 51-35-45-52.”

45-23-31 13-52 32-55-41-35-25 52-55 34-45-25-25.

WORD SEARCH

"STRANGE FIRE"

Aaron's sons, **Nadab** and **Abihu**, each took his **fire pan**, put fire in it, and put special **perfume** on it. They gave a fire that was **not holy** to the Lord because the Lord had not **told** them to do this. So the Lord sent out fire that burned them up and they **died** before the Lord. Then **Moses** said to **Aaron**, "This is what the Lord **meant** when He said, 'I will show **Myself** holy **among** those who are near Me. I will be **honored** in **front** of all the people.' " And Aaron said nothing.

LEVITICUS 10:1–3 NLV

SPOTTY HEADLINE

ISRA●L SAVE● FROM ●UD●MENT BY VARIOU● R●LERS

Hint: You won't find these guys (and one woman!) in a court of law.

___ ___ ___ ___ ___ ___

X	B	N	P	T	N	O	R	F	C
K	A	P	D	E	I	D	H	L	J
N	D	H	C	T	R	O	R	E	K
N	A	N	O	Z	N	F	L	S	L
O	N	L	B	O	G	A	U	Y	F
T	D	X	R	N	T	U	E	M	L
H	X	E	O	G	H	T	Z	M	E
O	D	M	F	I	R	E	P	A	N
L	A	V	B	L	S	E	S	O	M
Y	A	A	R	O	N	Z	V	M	G

DECODER

	1	2	3	4	5
1	N	U	T	E	P
2	O	Y	G	D	A
3	X	R	M	H	L
4	I	J	S	K	W
5	F	B	V	Z	C

REVELATION 7:16 NLV

"13-34-14-22 45-41-35-35 11-14-53-14-32 52-14 34-12-11-23-32-22 21-32 13-34-41-32-43-13-22 25-23-25-41-11. 13-34-14 43-12-11 21-32 25-11-22 52-12-32-11-41-11-23 34-14-25-13 45-41-35-35 11-21-13 43-34-41-11-14 24-21-45-11 21-11 13-34-14-33."

E
I
K
R
B
O
E
R
I

CLUES

A thorn (Ezekiel 28:24 KJV): B ___ ___ ___ ___

Found in your side (Genesis 2:22 KJV, SKJV): ___ ___ ___

Smashed; damaged (Exodus 32:19 NLV, SKJV): ___ ___ ___ ___ ___

STARS AND SAND

Because Sarah had **faith**, she was **able** to have a **child** **long after** she was past the **age** to have children. She had faith to **believe** that **God** would do what He **promised**. Abraham was **too old** to have children. But from this one man came a **family** with as **many** in it as the **stars** in the sky and as many as the **sand** by **the sea**.

HEBREWS 11:11–12 NLV

SPOTTY HEADLINE

MAN ●EPORDIZES LIV●S WIT● CHARIOT MANE●VERS

Hint: His driving was something else (2 Kings 9:20).

___ ___ ___ ___

B	N	T	F	T	O	O	O	L	D
D	R	E	T	F	A	G	N	O	L
D	E	S	I	M	O	R	P	E	B
C	H	I	L	D	B	A	L	T	E
W	Y	R	K	S	X	B	G	H	L
J	V	L	R	K	A	H	Y	E	I
B	S	A	I	R	R	T	N	S	E
M	T	A	G	M	N	I	A	E	V
S	J	O	N	J	A	A	M	A	E
J	D	T	W	D	T	F	Z	K	Y

Trickery

Genesis 27:35 SKJV

Sneaky Jacob used his father's blindness to steal something from his brother. Crack the code to find out what he took.

Jacob's mother (27:6)	17-23-14-9-4-27-5
"Come near and kiss me, my ________" (27:26 NLV)	11-2-21
"The ________ of my son is as the ________ of a field" (27:27 KJV; same word twice)	13-22-15-16-25
Found on the ground in the morning (27:28)	19-3-7
How Esau got his food (27:30)	12-28-8-20-6-1-10
"Esau gave out a loud ________" (27:38 NLV)	26-18-24

27-21-19 5-23 11-27-6-19, "24-2-28-17 14-18-2-20-12-9-17

26-27-22-15 7-6-20-12 19-3-26-3-6-20 27-21-19 5-27-11

20-27-4-23-1 27-7-27-24 24-2-28-18 14-16-15-13-11-6-8-10."

DECODER

	1	2	3	4	5
1	I	D	F	X	H
2	M	G	N	Y	K
3	T	S	O	L	R
4	B	J	V	U	C
5	E	P	A	Z	W

Proverbs 25:25 KJV

53-32 45-33-34-12 55-53-31-51-35-32 31-33 53 31-15-11-35-32-31-24 32-33-44-34, 32-33 11-32 22-33-33-12 23-51-55-32 13-35-33-21 53 13-53-35 45-33-44-23-31-35-24.

CROSSWORD

Gideon

Across

2. What Gideon saw miraculously come out of a rock (Judges 6:21)

4. Gideon tore down the altar of _________ (Judges 6:30)

7. Came to Gideon with an unexpected message (Judges 6:11)

8. God to Gideon: "You shall _________ Israel" (Judges 6:14 SKJV)

9. _________ hundred men remained in Gideon's army (Judges 7:6)

Down

1. Gideon was hiding wheat from the _________ (Judges 6:11)

3. "I will put a _________ of wool in the floor" (Judges 6:37 KJV)

5. "I am the _________ in my father's house" (Judges 6:15 SKJV)

6. "I dreamed. . .a cake of barley _________. . .came to a tent and struck it" (Judges 7:13 SKJV)

1
2
3
4
5
6
7
8
9

SCRAMBLED PLACE

RUN SAME JEWEL

Hint: Another name for heaven

___ ___ ___

___ ___ ___ ___ ___ ___ ___ ___ ___

Leafy Signs

"Now **learn** something from the **fig tree**. When the branch begins to **grow** and **puts out** its **leaves**, you know summer is **near**. In the same way, when you see **all** these things happen, you know the **Son of Man** is near. He is even at the **door**. For sure, I tell you, the **people** of this day will not **pass** away before all these things have **happened**. "**Heaven** and earth will pass away, but My **Words** will not pass away."

MARK 13:28–31 NLV

SPOTTY HEADLINE

GOD CRE●TES A
M●N FRO● ●UST

Hint: He was truly the first of his kind

___ ___ ___ ___

K	K	Z	K	P	A	S	S	Q	D
S	D	R	O	W	K	L	L	A	E
N	P	T	G	R	O	W	X	E	N
A	L	U	N	X	N	L	R	V	E
M	L	Y	T	E	M	T	K	L	P
F	E	N	A	S	G	R	P	F	P
O	A	R	L	I	O	O	O	D	A
N	V	A	F	K	E	U	W	O	H
O	E	E	K	P	T	Z	T	J	D
S	S	L	N	E	V	A	E	H	P

Brief But Amazing Faith

MATTHEW 14:29 NLV

Because Peter had faith, Jesus allowed him to do something extraordinary. . .for a few moments, at least. Crack the code to find out what it was.

"And when the evening ________, [Jesus] was there alone" (14:23 SKJV) 22-1-25-11

"Jesus. . .sent the ________ away" (14:22 NLV) 31-21-10-19-38-34

"The boat. . .was being ________ around by the waves" (14:24 NLV) 30-35-18-39-8-3

"The wind was strong ________ them" (14:24 NLV) 32-15-17-2-4-27-37

" ________ went unto them, walking on the sea" (14:25 KJV) 14-12-16-7-29

"And [the disciples] cried out in ________" (14:26 SKJV) 36-24-13-26

[Jesus said], " ________ hope. It is I" (14:27 NLV) 5-9-28-23

"Lord, if it be thou, ________ me come unto thee" (14:28 KJV) 33-20-6

14-11-27-7-16 29-13-20-6, "22-39-25-21!" 31-11-30-34-26

15-10-37 39-7-5 10-36 30-35-24 33-10-32-5 1-3-6

8-1-38-28-23-6 10-3 5-35-34 8-1-37-11-18 5-39

14-11-27-7-29.

BIBLE DIAMOND

R
S
A
I
I
E
P
L
E

CLUES

Jacob's new name (Genesis 32:28):

___ ___ ___ ___ ___ ___

A hot coal touched this on Isaiah

(Isaiah 6:6–7): ___ ___ ___

Old word for an instrument; it's also found under your sink

(1 Samuel 10:5 KJV, SKJV): ___ ___ ___ ___

Bee Stings

"I will send My **fear** before you and will destroy all the people to whom you shall come, and I will make all your **enemies turn** their **backs** to you. And I will send **hornets** before you, which shall **drive** out the **Hivite**, the **Canaanite**, and the **Hittite** from before you. I will not drive them out from before you in <u>**one year**</u>, lest the land become **desolate** and the **beasts** of the field **multiply** against you."

EXODUS 23:27–29 SKJV

SPOTTY HEADLINE

IS●AEL ●ORN FROM ●W●LVE FACT●ON●

Hint: They were an ancient version of states.

___ ___ ___ ___ ___ ___

X	B	T	H	I	T	T	I	T	E
D	R	A	F	N	Z	L	K	W	D
E	R	H	C	F	N	S	G	R	M
S	A	O	C	K	E	B	I	R	U
O	E	R	H	I	S	V	X	A	L
L	Y	N	M	R	E	P	Y	E	T
A	E	E	N	T	U	R	N	F	I
T	N	T	S	T	S	A	E	B	P
E	O	S	E	T	I	V	I	H	L
E	T	I	N	A	A	N	A	C	Y

DECODER

	1	2	3	4	5
1	P	C	K	R	A
2	H	J	T	X	B
3	L	D	M	V	Y
4	O	S	E	F	U
5	W	I	G	N	Z

Romans 2:11 NLV

53-41-32 32-41-43-42 54-41-23 42-21-41-51 44-15-34-41-14

23-41 41-54-43 33-15-54 33-41-14-43 23-21-15-54 23-41

15-54-41-23-21-43-14.

Miraculous Escape!

Exodus 14:22 KJV

Trapped between an angry army and a raging sea, it seemed the Israelites were doomed. Crack the code to find out how they escaped.

"The children of Israel went _________ with a high hand" (14:8 SKJV) 28-11-7

"The _________ pursued after them" (14:9 KJV) 12-31-14-33-1-32-21-19-23

"And Moses said to the people, 'Do not _________'" (14:13 SKJV) 26-22-5-13

"The pillar of the _________ went from before their face" (14:19 KJV) 3-29-10-9-18

"And the LORD [sent] a strong east _________" (14:21 SKJV) 6-20-15-27

"All Pharaoh's horses, his chariots, and his _________" (14:23 SKJV) 4-30-16-8-2-25-17-24

21-19-18 7-4-12 3-4-32-29-27-13-22-19 28-26

20-23-13-5-17-15 6-22-15-7 32-15-1-28 7-4-2

25-20-27-23-1 10-26 1-4-2 23-22-21 9-33-28-15 1-4-22

18-13-14 31-13-28-11-15-18.

Heaven

Across

1. "And he shewed me a pure river of water of life, clear as _________" (Revelation 22:1 KJV)

4. "I am going away to make a _________ for you" (John 14:2 NLV)

5. "Lay not up for yourselves _________ upon earth" (Matthew 6:19 KJV)

8. "In my Father's house are many _________" (John 14:2 KJV)

Down

2. "Set your affection on things _________" (Colossians 3:2 KJV)

3. "The gate is _________ . . .that leads to life" (Matthew 7:14 SKJV)

6. "Willing to be _________ from the body and to be present with the Lord" (2 Corinthians 5:8 SKJV)

7. "And, behold, there are _________ which shall be first" (Luke 13:30 KJV)

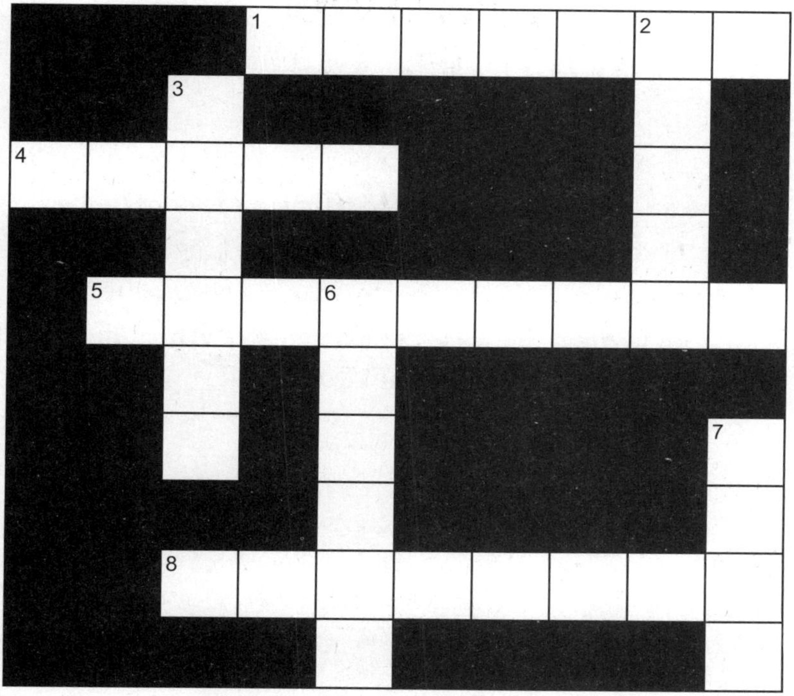
1
2
3
4
5
6
7
8

SPOTTY HEADLINE

G●D●ON DEFE●T●
THESE ENE●●ES W●TH
●HREE HUN●RED ME●

Hint: Their country rhymes with "Gideon."

___ ___ ___ ___ ___ ___ ___ ___ ___ ___

ONE HOT SUMMER DAY. . .

The **Lord** showed Himself to **Abraham** by the **oak trees** of **Mamre**, as he sat at the **tent door** in the **heat** of the day. Abraham **looked** up and saw **three men** standing in **front** of him. When he saw them, he **ran** from the tent door to **meet** them. He put his **face** to the **ground**.

GENESIS 18:1–2 NLV

SPOTTY HEADLINE

P●UL ENDS UP ON ●YS●ERIOUS IS●●ND

Hint: It's in the Mediterranean Sea.

___ ___ ___ ___ ___

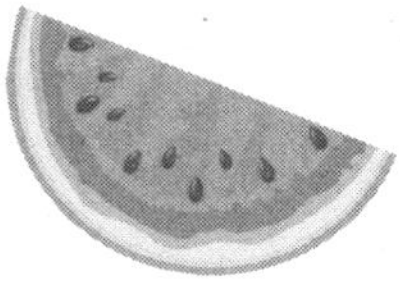

T	C	D	E	K	O	O	L	B	N
L	N	Q	P	V	N	M	Q	T	E
W	Y	O	W	A	A	G	G	E	M
Y	J	M	R	H	Z	D	R	N	E
F	T	G	A	F	Y	R	O	T	E
F	A	R	M	H	C	O	U	D	R
J	B	C	E	A	R	L	N	O	H
A	L	A	E	W	M	M	D	O	T
J	T	M	E	E	T	R	G	R	N
R	O	A	K	T	R	E	E	S	R

	1	2	3	4	5
1	Z	W	Y	P	A
2	K	F	D	J	Q
3	L	V	S	U	M
4	N	T	R	B	G
5	H	O	C	I	E

1 Corinthians 15:22 KJV

22-52-43 15-33 54-41 15-23-15-35 15-31-31 23-54-55,

55-32-55-41 33-52 54-41 53-51-43-54-33-42 33-51-15-31-31

15-31-31 44-55 35-15-23-55 15-31-54-32-55.

BIBLE DIAMOND

V
E O
L H L
S Y
E

CLUES

Set apart (Leviticus 11:44): H ___ ___ ___

Word of agreement (2 Corinthians 1:18 NLV, SKJV):

___ ___ ___

Used for digging (Isaiah 30:24 KJV, SKJV):

___ ___ ___ ___ ___ ___

Getting It Done

The Lord will not let those who are **right** with Him go **hungry**, but He puts to one **side** the **desire** of the **sinful**. He who works with a **lazy** hand is **poor**, but the hand of the **hard worker** brings **riches**. A son who gathers in **summer** is **wise**, but a son who sleeps during **gathering** time brings **shame**.

PROVERBS 10:3–5 NLV

SCRAMBLED THING

AH FIG HUES

Hint: It swallowed a prophet

___ ___ ___ ___ ___ ___ ___ ___ ___

H	S	S	I	D	E	R	O	O	P
A	G	E	T	D	S	H	A	M	E
R	A	R	H	H	E	D	K	R	C
D	T	E	G	C	K	S	Y	V	F
W	H	M	I	S	I	R	I	E	Y
O	E	M	R	I	G	R	S	R	L
R	R	U	X	N	N	I	X	A	E
K	I	S	U	F	W	V	Z	X	V
E	N	H	P	U	X	Y	N	N	L
R	G	Q	S	L	E	E	P	S	N

SAUL'S CONVERSION

ACTS 9:4 SKJV

Saul went from Christ-hating Pharisee to beloved apostle in no time flat. Crack the code to find out what caused this dramatic change.

Saul asked the high _________ for letters (9:1–2) 47-5-27-29-41-19

Jewish places of worship (9:2) 43-1-40-45-26-32-17-11-22-34

Paul was headed toward _________ (9:3) 30-2-25-24-15-16-21-39

"Arise, and go into the _________" (9:6 SKJV) 36-44-12-14

"And for three days he was _________ sight" (9:9 SKJV) 18-6-7-28-37-31-9

"He is a chosen _________ for Me" (9:15 SKJV) 13-46-42-23-3-4

"I will show him how much he must _________ for My name's sake" (9:16 SKJV) 33-10-38-20-8-35

45-40-30 28-29 38-22-4-4 19-32 12-28-46 46-2-35-9-28

2-40-30 28-3-24-35-30 45 13-37-27-36-8

43-24-14-44-40-17 12-37 28-6-25, "15-2-11-4, 33-45-11-4,

18-28-14 45-35-29 14-37-21

47-46-5-43-8-16-31-19-44-40-17 25-29?"

DECODER

	1	2	3	4	5
1	O	U	B	G	E
2	N	W	I	R	C
3	D	H	X	P	M
4	Y	Z	A	J	F
5	S	V	T	L	K

Philippians 2:10 KJV

53-32-43-53 43-53 53-32-15 21-43-35-15 11-45

44-15-51-12-51 15-52-15-24-41 55-21-15-15 51-32-11-12-54-31

13-11-22, 11-45 53-32-23-21-14-51 23-21 32-15-43-52-15-21,

43-21-31 53-32-23-21-14-51 23-21 15-43-24-53-32, 43-21-31

53-32-23-21-14-51 12-21-31-15-24 53-32-15 15-43-24-53-32.

FRUITS

Across

4. "Bring forth therefore fruits worthy of ________" (Luke 3:8 KJV)

5. "He said to the tree, 'No fruit will ever ________ on you again' " (Matthew 21:19 NLV)

8. "Every tree that does not give ________ fruit is. . .thrown into the fire" (Matthew 3:10 NLV)

Down

1. "I am the true ________, and my Father is the husbandman" (John 15:1 KJV)

2. "A good ________ cannot have bad fruit" (Matthew 7:18 NLV)

3. Love and joy are fruits of the ________ (Galatians 5:22 KJV)

6. "But the ________ that is from above is. . . .full of mercy and good fruits" (James 3:17 KJV)

7. "All the trees of the ________ dry up" (Joel 1:12 NLV)

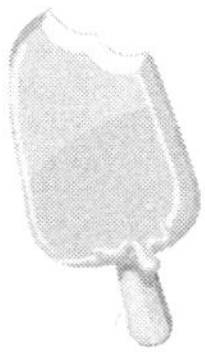

1
2
3
4
5
6
7
8

SPOTTY HEADLINE

L●●ELY BIR● DESC●NDS

Hint: This beautiful creature rested on Jesus.

___ ___ ___ ___

WORD SEARCH

After the Harvest

Woe is me! For I am like when they have gathered the summer fruits, like the **harvest** of the **grapes**. There is no **cluster** **to eat**. My **soul** desired the **first**-ripe fruit. The **good man** has **perished** from the earth, and there is no one **upright** among men. They all **lie in wait** for **blood**. Every man **hunts** his brother with a **net**.

Micah 7:1–2 SKJV

SPOTTY HEADLINE

GOD PROMIS●S ET●R●●L ●OME FOR BELIE●ERS

Hint: Accept Jesus to live there with Him.

___ ___ ___ ___ ___ ___

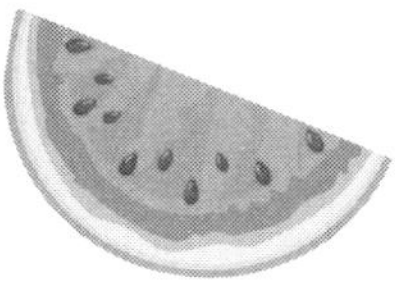

G	O	O	D	M	A	N	T	F	P
H	T	S	R	I	F	S	I	Y	E
D	G	R	A	P	E	S	A	H	R
Y	O	T	C	V	M	C	W	H	I
T	E	O	R	Z	S	L	N	U	S
N	O	A	L	O	I	U	I	N	H
F	H	E	U	B	E	S	E	T	E
R	R	L	A	D	O	T	I	S	D
M	G	P	N	T	W	E	L	B	P
L	J	T	H	G	I	R	P	U	N

A DARK DAY FOR JOSEPH

GENESIS 37:24 KJV

Driven by jealousy, Joseph's brothers briefly trapped him in a very unpleasant place. Crack the code to find out where it was.

"They _________ against [Joseph] to slay him" (37:18 KJV) 14-17-7-3-20-33-11-1-21

"A _________ of Ishmeelites came from Gilead" (37:25 KJV) 32-15-9-25-5-26-12

"Then there passed by Midianites _________" (37:28 KJV, SKJV) 24-27-13-4-29-34-23-8-16-28-30

A young goat (37:31 KJV, SKJV) 18-31-10

"Thus his father _________ for him" (37:35 KJV, SKJV) 19-6-22-2

5-23-10 2-29-28-12 8-17-15-18 29-33-9, 5-30-10

32-34-3-2 29-31-24 31-7-2-15 34 20-31-2: 5-7-10 2-29-1

22-31-2 19-5-3 28-24-20-8-12, 2-29-28-11-28 19-5-3 30-15

19-5-2-6-13 33-23 31-2.

H
A
C
O
T
U
B
O
M

CLUES

A grave (Matthew 27:60 KJV, SKJV): T ___ ___ ___

Where Jesus slept during a storm

(Matthew 8:24 NLV): ___ ___ ___ ___

One of the five senses

(Mark 5:28): ___ ___ ___ ___ ___

Ripe for Disaster

This is what the **Lord God showed** me: There was a **basket** of **summer fruit**. And the Lord said, "What do you see, **Amos**?" I said, "A basket of summer fruit." Then the Lord said to me, "**The end** has come for My **people Israel**. I **will not change** My **mind** again about **punishing** them."

AMOS 8:1–2 NLV

SPOTTY HEADLINE

PRO●HE● JOHN GET●
W●●ER-●ASED N●CKNAME

Hint: Probably because he was in the river so often!

___ ___ ___ ___ ___ ___ ___

X	T	C	Z	S	D	D	L	Y	N
P	M	N	H	E	U	A	N	L	T
U	X	D	W	A	M	M	D	I	F
N	M	O	B	O	N	L	M	L	M
I	H	G	S	X	Z	G	Y	E	K
S	F	D	B	A	S	K	E	T	R
H	R	R	X	P	E	O	P	L	E
I	U	O	T	O	N	L	L	I	W
N	I	L	D	N	E	E	H	T	T
G	T	L	E	A	R	S	I	L	C

DECODER

	1	2	3	4	5
1	P	B	L	K	E
2	W	R	H	X	G
3	M	Y	A	Z	U
4	O	N	F	D	V
5	S	C	I	T	J

Job 12:13 NLV

"21-53-54-23 25-41-44 33-22-15 21-53-51-44-41-31 33-42-44 51-54-22-15-42-25-54-23. 21-53-51-15 21-41-22-44-51 33-42-44 35-42-44-15-22-51-54-33-42-44-53-42-25 12-15-13-41-42-25 54-41 23-53-31."

DECODER

	1	2	3	4	5
1	U	O	W	P	B
2	D	K	H	L	X
3	I	T	G	C	S
4	V	A	F	M	R
5	Z	N	J	E	Y

MATTHEW 5:5 KJV

15-24-54-35-35-54-21 42-45-54 32-23-54 44-54-54-22:

43-12-45 32-23-54-55 35-23-42-24-24

31-52-23-54-45-31-32 32-23-54 54-42-45-32-23.

BALAAM AND HIS DONKEY

Across

1. "The __________ of the Lord stood in the way against him" (Numbers 22:22 NLV)
3. The donkey "lay down __________ Balaam" (Numbers 22:27 NLV)
5. "So Balaam rose up. . .and went with the princes of __________" (Numbers 22:21 KJV)
6. What the angel was carrying (Numbers 22:23)
8. The donkey "crushed Balaam's __________ against" the wall (Numbers 22:25 NLV)

Down

2. The path was __________ (Numbers 22:24 NLV)
4. "The donkey turned off the __________ and went into the field" (Numbers 22:23 NLV)
6. "And the Lord opened the __________ of the donkey" (Numbers 22:28 NLV)
7. "Balaam was angry and hit the donkey with his __________" (Numbers 22:27 NLV)

1
2
3
4
5
6
7
8

SPOTTY HEADLINE

F●ERY MOUNTAI●
D●SPL●YS GOD'● GLORY

Hint: Also the name of a peninsula.

____ ____ ____ ____ ____

For the Birds

And the word of the LORD came to him, saying, "**Get away** from here and turn **eastward**, and **hide** yourself by the **brook Cherith**, which is before the Jordan. And it shall be that you shall drink from the brook, and I have **commanded** the **ravens** to **feed** you there." So he went and did according to the word of the LORD, for he went and **dwelled** by the brook Cherith, which is **before** the Jordan. And the ravens brought him **bread** and **meat** in the **morning** and bread and meat in the **evening**, and he drank from the brook.

1 KINGS 17:2–6 SKJV

SCRAMBLED PERSON

SINK MOON LOG

Hint: A really smart guy.

___ ___ ___ ___

___ ___ ___ ___ ___ ___ ___

D	E	D	N	A	M	M	O	C	D
V	H	I	D	E	K	R	L	R	Y
B	K	V	M	G	A	M	A	Y	D
M	R	X	X	V	H	W	R	A	C
E	Y	O	E	D	T	M	E	W	H
A	N	N	O	S	E	R	R	A	E
T	S	H	A	K	B	E	O	T	R
D	W	E	L	L	E	D	F	E	I
M	O	R	N	I	N	G	E	G	T
G	N	I	N	E	V	E	B	H	H

ACROSTIC

THE UNWILLING PROPHET

JONAH 1:2 KJV

Jonah was God's prophet, but he had a really tough time obeying one of God's commands. Crack the code to find out what it was.

Jonah tried fleeing to ________ (1:3)
32-27-41-48-29-20-24-2

"The weeds were ________ about my head" (2:5 KJV, SKJV)
6-16-9-22-38-13-25

"I went down to the bottoms of the ________" (2:6 KJV, SKJV)
26-5-1-34-46-49-19-3-30

"The earth with her ________ was about me for ever"(2:6 KJV)
11-36-43-14

"I will sacrifice unto thee with the voice of ________" (2:9 KJV)
8-23-35-4-40-17-15-42-45-10-28-47

Judgment would happen in ________ days (3:4)
39-44-21-12-33

Jonah sat on the east side of the ________ (4:5)
7-18-37-31

27-16-20-48-13, 15-5 32-44 34-10-28-13-45-13-2,

46-23-9-12 47-21-13-36-37 7-19-8-33, 49-4-25 7-16-31

35-47-27-18-34-48-8 18-37; 39-5-16 32-2-13-19-43

6-42-7-40-13-25-3-13-24-30 18-14 7-5-26-13 1-22

11-13-39-5-21-13 26-13.

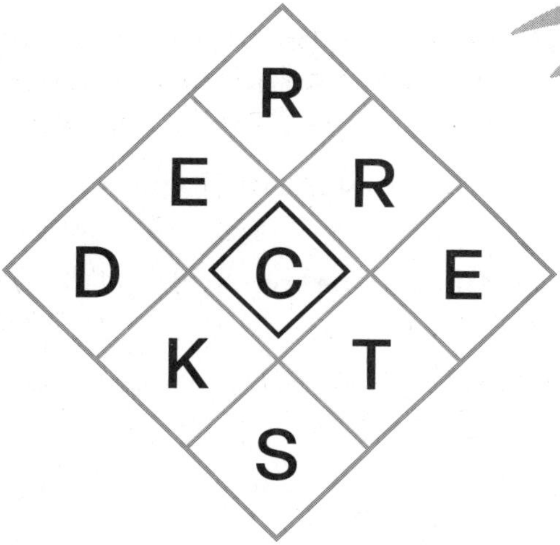
R
E
R
D
C
E
K
T
S

CLUES

Island Paul visited (Acts 27:21): C ___ ___ ___ ___

Messed up; made a mistake (Leviticus 5:18 KJV, SKJV):

___ ___ ___ ___ ___

Short word for "decorates" (Isaiah 61:10 SKJV):

___ ___ ___ ___ ___

WORD SEARCH

"Death Valley"

He led me **around** the **valley**. I saw there were very **many** bones, and they were **very** dry. He said to me, "Son of man, can these bones **live**?" I answered, "O **Lord** God, **only** You know that." He said to me, "**Speak** in My **name** over these bones. Say to them, 'O **dry bones**, **hear** the Word of the Lord.' This is what the Lord God says to these bones: 'I will make breath come into you, and you will **come to life**. I will **join** you **together**, make flesh grow back on you, **cover** you with skin, and put breath in you to make you come to life. Then you will know that I am the Lord.' "

EZEKIEL 37:2–6 NLV

SPOTTY HEADLINE

GO● PLANTS A P●AC●FUL GARDE●

Hint: It was paradise. . .for a while.

___ ___ ___ ___

K	A	E	P	S	R	D	S	C	X
E	X	V	R	P	Y	D	E	O	T
K	M	A	E	E	G	N	N	M	O
C	E	A	L	R	C	U	O	E	G
H	O	L	N	X	Y	O	B	T	E
R	A	V	F	R	N	R	Y	O	T
V	N	V	E	L	L	A	R	L	H
M	A	N	Y	R	I	N	D	I	E
L	O	R	D	P	V	R	K	F	R
P	J	O	I	N	E	X	R	E	W

DECODER

	1	2	3	4	5
1	C	Y	U	D	V
2	M	R	J	S	N
3	B	F	T	A	G
4	L	W	K	X	I
5	P	E	Z	H	O

EPHESIANS 6:2 KJV

54-55-25-55-13-22 33-54-12 32-34-33-54-52-22 34-25-14

21-55-33-54-52-22; 42-54-45-11-54 45-24 33-54-52

32-45-22-24-33 11-55-21-21-34-25-14-21-52-25-33

42-45-33-54 51-22-55-21-45-24-52.

Cave-Dwelling Fear

1 Kings 19:1 KJV

Fearful of the evil queen Jezebel's wrath, Elijah ran for his life and hid in a cave. Crack the code to find out what had made the queen so mad.

"He. . .went a day's journey into the ________" (19:4 KJV, SKJV) 4-14-5-15-11-26-10-33-7-6

"Take my life. For I am not ________ than my fathers" (19:4 NLV) 12-29-17-20-34-30

Elijah "________ under a juniper tree" (19:5 KJV, SKJV) 25-21-22-18-28

"What doest thou here, ________?" (19:9 KJV) 3-16-31-32-23-1

"I have been very ________ for the Lord God of hosts" (19:14 SKJV) 8-24-13-19-2-27-9

23-10-15 13-1-23-12 28-2-16-15 32-3-8-11-12-33-5 13-19-21

17-1-23-20 22-21-14-32-13-1 1-13-15 15-2-10-24, 23-10-15

4-31-28-1-23-19 1-2-4 1-3 1-13-15 25-19-23-14-10 13-21-5

28-1-11 18-26-2-18-1-33-28-9 4-31-20-1 28-1-24

25-4-2-30-15.

SiN

Across

1. "Sin must not have __________ over you" (Romans 6:14 NLV)

3. "They that are in the flesh cannot __________ God" (Romans 8:8 KJV)

4. "Love covers the __________ of sins" (1 Peter 4:8 SKJV)

7. "For all have sinned, and come __________ of the glory of God" (Romans 3:23 KJV)

Down

2. "__________, and turn yourselves from all your transgressions" (Ezekiel 18:30 KJV)

4. "Out of the same __________ proceeds blessing and cursing" (James 3:10 SKJV)

5. "The sting of death is sin; and the strength of sin is the __________" (1 Corinthians 15:56 KJV)

6. "The wages of sin is __________" (Romans 6:23 KJV)

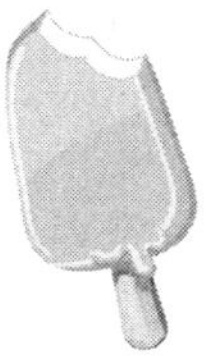

1
2
3
4
5
6
7

SPOTTY HEADLINE

P●OP●ET ●AILED ●ND ●GNOR●D IN HIS ●IS●RY

Hint: He's called the "weeping prophet" for a reason

___ ___ ___ ___ ___ ___ ___ ___

FACTS OF FAITH

For I **delivered** to you first of all what I also received, that **Christ** died for our sins according to the **scriptures**, and that He was **buried**, and that He **rose** again the third day according to the scriptures, and that He was seen by **Cephas**, then by the **twelve**. After that He was seen by more than five **hundred** brothers at once, of whom the **majority** remain to the present, but some have fallen **asleep**. After that He was seen by **James**, then by all the **apostles**. And last of all, as by one born out of due time, He was also seen by me.

1 CORINTHIANS 15:3–8 SKJV

SPOTTY HEADLINE

E●IJAH ●HALL●NGES P●OPHETS ●TOP A ●OUNTAIN

Hint: Sadly, it isn't as delicious as it sounds.

___ ___ ___ ___ ___ ___

N	R	P	F	N	C	N	R	D	P
Y	S	W	E	E	C	T	O	E	M
A	E	B	P	E	S	V	S	R	A
P	M	H	U	I	L	N	E	E	J
O	A	N	R	R	B	S	H	V	O
S	J	H	Y	M	I	N	A	I	R
T	C	B	B	D	X	E	T	L	I
L	E	V	L	E	W	T	D	E	T
E	H	U	N	D	R	E	D	D	Y
S	C	R	I	P	T	U	R	E	S

DECODER

	1	2	3	4	5
1	S	K	O	G	M
2	B	T	H	J	L
3	P	X	A	I	R
4	W	Z	V	Y	N
5	D	C	E	U	F

1 Thessalonians 5:2 KJV

55-13-35 44-13-54-35-11-53-25-43-53-11 12-45-13-41

31-53-35-55-53-52-22-25-44 22-23-33-22 22-23-53

51-33-44 13-55 22-23-53 25-13-35-51 11-13

52-13-15-53-22-23 33-11 33 22-23-34-53-55 34-45

22-23-53 45-34-14-23-22.

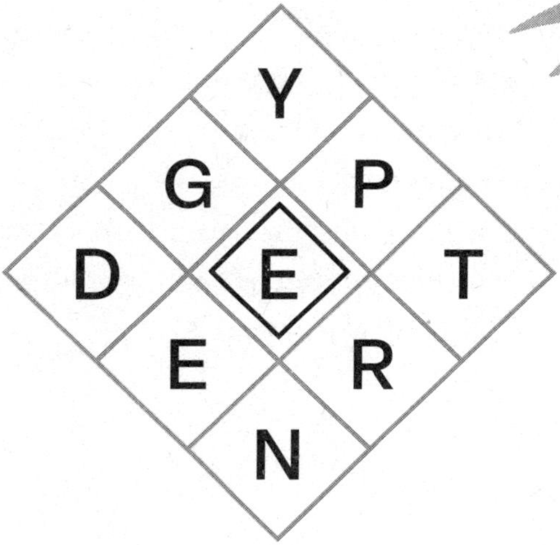
Y
G
P
D
E
T
E
R
N

CLUES

Where Joseph ended up (Genesis 37:28):

E ____ ____ ____ ____

Where fruit is found (Genesis 1:11): ____ ____ ____ ____

Lost garden of paradise (Genesis 2:8):

____ ____ ____ ____

THE END OF TIME

And the **angel** that I saw stand on the sea and on the earth **lifted up** his **hand** to heaven, and **swore** by Him who **lives forever** and ever, who **created** heaven and the **things** that are **in it**, and the earth and the things that are in it, and **the sea** and the things that are in it, that there should **no longer** be **time**.

REVELATION 10:5–6 SKJV

SPOTTY HEADLINE

GOD'S DI●I●ITY ●YMBOLIZ●D IN A NUMB●R

Hint: God built it into creation week.

___ ___ ___ ___ ___

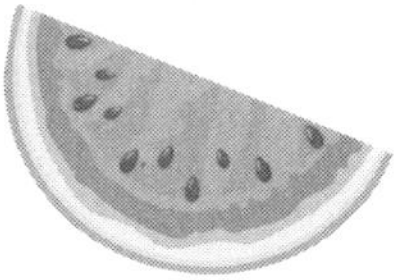

C	D	E	T	A	E	R	C	T	C
R	E	G	N	O	L	O	N	J	Q
B	F	T	S	Z	R	E	D	P	P
M	O	H	R	W	M	K	U	Z	L
L	R	I	T	I	O	D	L	I	A
L	E	N	T	I	E	R	V	X	E
E	V	G	V	T	N	E	E	J	S
G	E	S	F	N	S	I	D	R	E
N	R	I	D	H	A	N	D	M	H
A	L	L	M	Y	B	F	K	Y	T

WATER INTO WINE

JOHN 2:2 KJV

Jesus performed one of His most famous miracles in Cana. Crack the code to find out why He was there.

Where Cana was located (2:1)
23-36-24-15-25-14-11

"_________, what have I to do with thee?" (2:4 KJV)
2-35-8-5-9

"My _________ has not yet come" (2:4 SKJV)
22-3-12-13

"Six stone water _________ were there" (2:6 NLV)
16-18-32-34

"Everyone puts out his _________ wine first" (2:10 NLV)
37-29-21-10

"You have kept the _________ wine until now!" (2:10 NLV)
19-31-4-7

"After this he went down to _________" (2:12 KJV)
30-33-1-17-20-28-27-6-26

5-9-7 37-35-10-22 16-14-34-12-21 2-5-34 30-36-25-24-11-7,

18-28-7 22-15-34 7-15-21-30-15-1-24-29-34, 10-4 10-22-29

8-33-13-32-15-27-19-17.

DECODER

	1	2	3	4	5
1	D	A	C	O	J
2	I	T	N	K	B
3	X	S	G	Y	L
4	U	F	R	H	M
5	V	E	Z	P	W

Colossians 1:15 SKJV

44-52 21-32 22-44-52 21-45-12-33-52 14-42

22-44-52 21-23-51-21-32-21-25-35-52 33-14-11, 22-44-52

42-21-43-32-22-25-14-43-23 14-42 52-51-52-43-34

13-43-52-12-22-41-43-52.

Forgiveness

Across

1. "And forgive us our debts, as we forgive our ________" (Matthew 6:12 KJV)

3. "Love your ________, bless them that curse you" (Matthew 5:44 KJV)

5. "If we ________ our sins, he is faithful and just to forgive us our sins" (1 John 1:9 KJV)

7. "Forgive other people just as ________ forgave you" (Ephesians 4:32 NLV)

8. "Hatred stirreth up strifes: but ________ covereth all sins" (Proverbs 10:12 KJV)

Down

2. " ________ are the merciful: for they shall obtain mercy" (Matthew 5:7 KJV)

4. "Father, forgive them; for they ________ not what they do" (Luke 23:34 KJV)

6. "Anyone of you who is without sin can throw the first ________" (John 8:7 NLV)

1
2
3
4
5
6
7
8

SPOTTY HEADLINE

MOS● SO●E●OW OV●R●OOK
J●SUS' ●IRT● IN ME●K TOWN

Hint: Well, it was just a "little town."

___ ___ ___ ___ ___ ___ ___ ___ ___

Forever Day

And I saw no **temple** in it, for the Lord God **Almighty** and the **Lamb** are its temple. And the **city** had no need of the sun or of the **moon** to **shine** in it, for the **glory of God** illuminated it, and the Lamb is its **light**. And the **nations** of those who are **saved** shall walk in its light, and the **kings** of the earth bring their glory and **honor** into it. And its **gates** shall not be shut at all by day, for there shall be **no night** there.

REVELATION 21:22–25 SKJV

SCRAMBLED COMMAND

NONE GIVE HOT

Hint: God gave it to Jonah.

___ ___ ___ ___

___ ___ ___ ___ ___ ___ ___

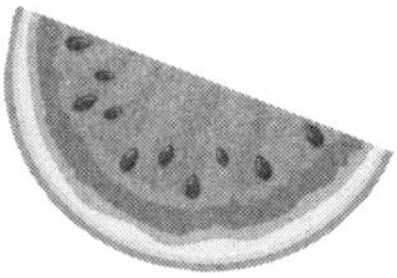

D	O	G	F	O	Y	R	O	L	G
L	A	M	B	R	K	D	K	Y	E
C	M	O	N	L	E	M	T	R	L
S	G	O	P	V	T	H	J	T	P
N	A	N	A	M	G	H	M	H	M
O	T	S	C	I	H	S	G	G	E
I	E	R	M	I	H	O	C	I	T
T	S	L	J	I	T	F	N	N	L
A	A	N	N	L	R	Y	F	O	H
N	D	E	K	I	N	G	S	N	R

Sermon on the Mount

Matthew 6:33 SKJV

In Matthew 5–7, Jesus gave an unforgettable sermon about how we're supposed to live. Crack the code to find out what our focus in life should be.

"_________ are the poor in spirit:
for theirs is the kingdom of heaven"
(5:3 KJV) 26-5-36-24-33-29-30

"You are the salt of the _________"
(5:13 NLV, SKJV) 35-9-8-23-32

"Thy _________ come, Thy will be done"
(6:10 KJV) 27-18-20-21-17-3-16

"The light of the _________ is the eye" (6:22 KJV)
22-12-19-13

Word for clothing in the KJV (6:28)
7-2-6-28-31-25-1

"Ye shall know them by their _________"
(7:16 KJV) 11-14-34-15-10-4

"26-34-23 24-29-35-27 11-18-8-33-1 10-32-35

27-6-25-21-30-12-28 3-11 21-3-17 9-20-30 32-15-4

7-18-21-32-23-36-3-34-4-20-31-4-24, 9-25-30 2-5-5

10-32-31-33-35 1-32-18-25-21-33 4-32-9-5-5 22-35

2-19-17-36-30 1-12 13-3-34."

W
A
L
E
L
S
K
N
A

CLUES

Received, then shared, by Moses (Joshua 8:31): L ____ ____

Rebuilt by Nehemiah (Nehemiah 2:13):

____ ____ ____ ____ ____

Snuck into a garden (Genesis 3:1 NLV):

____ ____ ____ ____ ____

WHAT A SCORCHER!

But the **day** of the Lord will come as a **thief** in the **night**, in which the heavens shall **pass** away with a great **noise**, and the **elements** shall **melt** with **fervent** heat. The earth also and the **works** that are in it shall be **burned** up. Since all these things shall be **dissolved**, what manner of persons ought you to be in all **holy** conduct and **godliness**. . . ?

2 PETER 3:10–11 SKJV

SPOTTY HEADLINE

STR●●GE FOO● ●●ICKLY
F●L●S TO E●RTH ●N
E●RLY ●OR●I●G

Hint: Bread and birds.

___ ___ ___ ___ ___   ___ ___ ___

___ ___ ___ ___ ___

K	T	B	U	R	N	E	D	Q	T
S	S	E	N	I	L	D	O	G	N
D	E	V	L	O	S	S	I	D	E
S	T	N	E	M	E	L	E	Y	V
N	R	N	I	G	H	T	T	A	R
O	Y	Y	R	W	W	P	F	D	E
I	M	L	O	P	M	E	A	G	F
S	R	R	O	E	I	T	W	S	Q
E	K	D	L	H	M	K	H	X	S
S	P	T	T	T	N	T	T	N	N

	1	2	3	4	5
1	T	O	U	I	D
2	Y	N	E	P	F
3	R	A	C	L	B
4	G	M	H	K	W
5	S	X	V	Z	J

REVELATION 21:7 KJV

43-23 11-43-32-11 12-53-23-31-33-12-42-23-11-43

51-43-32-34-34 14-22-43-23-31-14-11 32-34-34

11-43-14-22-41-51; 32-22-15 14 45-14-34-34 35-23

43-14-51 41-12-15, 32-22-15 43-23 51-43-32-34-34 35-23

42-21 51-12-22.

	1	2	3	4	5
1	W	Y	J	M	X
2	Z	A	G	K	N
3	P	D	B	H	L
4	T	R	E	C	I
5	V	U	S	F	O

GENESIS 1:1 KJV

45-25 41-34-43 33-43-23-45-25-25-45-25-23 23-55-32 44-42-43-22-41-43-32 41-34-43 34-43-22-51-43-25 22-25-32 41-34-43 43-22-42-41-34.

CROSSWORD

Trees

Across

1. "There were twelve wells of water and seventy _________ trees in Elim" (Numbers 33:9 NLV)

5. "Of the tree of the _________ of good and evil, you shall not eat of it" (Genesis 2:17 SKJV)

6. "Those who are right with God will grow like a green _________" (Proverbs 11:28 NLV)

8. "The righteous shall. . .grow like a _________ in Lebanon" (Psalm 92:12 KJV)

Down

1. "He shall be like a tree _________ by the waters" (Jeremiah 17:8 SKJV)

2. "Then the trees of the _________ will sing for joy before the Lord" (1 Chronicles 16:33 NLV)

3. "The tree of _________ also in the midst of the garden" (Genesis 2:9 KJV)

4. "I am like a green _________ tree in the house of God" (Psalm 52:8 KJV)

7. "They acted like men taking up _________ against a group of trees" (Psalm 74:5 NLV)

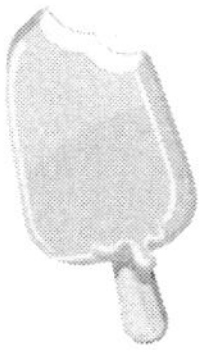

1
2
3
4
5
6
7
8

SPOTTY HEADLINE

LEFT-●ANDED JU●G●
T●RNS ASSASSIN

Hint: The evil king Eglon never saw it coming (Judges 3:21).

____ ____ ____ ____

Cold Glass of Water

"He who receives you **receives Me**, and he who receives Me receives Him who **sent** Me. He who receives a **prophet** in the name of a prophet shall receive a prophet's **reward**. And he who receives a **righteous** man in the name of a righteous man shall receive a righteous man's reward. And **whoever** gives to one of these **little ones** even a **cup** of cold **water** to **drink** in the name of a **disciple**, truly, I say to you, he shall in no way **lose** his reward."

MATTHEW 10:42–45 SKJV

SPOTTY HEADLINE

L●T●LE SHEP●ERD
FE●R●ESSLY ●PPOSES
THIS ●IANT

Hint: David took him out with a sling and stone.

___ ___ ___ ___ ___ ___ ___

S	E	N	O	E	L	T	T	I	L
R	M	R	R	R	Q	K	T	L	K
I	S	E	K	Z	E	N	K	O	R
G	E	T	L	N	E	W	W	S	M
H	V	A	D	S	I	H	A	E	K
T	I	W	C	K	O	R	P	R	V
E	E	T	F	E	M	Q	D	U	D
O	C	K	V	R	D	P	R	K	C
U	E	E	P	R	O	P	H	E	T
S	R	D	I	S	C	I	P	L	E

DAVID AND GOLIATH

1 SAMUEL 17:54 KJV

David, little more than a shepherd boy, faced down a giant Philistine warrior. Crack the code to find out who came out alive.

The Philistines gathered. . .at Socoh, which belongs to _________" (17:1 SKJV) 34-28-12-37-10

"The weight of [Goliath's] coat was five thousand _________ of brass" (17:5 KJV) 16-23-22-27-8-30-1

"Why have you. . .set your battle in _________?" (17:8 SKJV) 14-21-9-36-33-7-38-35-4

"David. . .left the _________ with a keeper" (17:20 SKJV) 3-2-20-5-6

"Your servant has killed both the lion and the _________ " (17:36 NLV) 29-11-24-15

"[Goliath] hath defied the armies of the _________ God" (17:36 KJV) 13-26-19-32-25-18

"Am I a _________, that you come to me with sticks?" (17:43 NLV) 39-31-17

37-4-12 39-33-19-38-12 7-21-35-27 7-10-22 23-8-24-39

21-14 7-2-5 6-2-26-13-32-16-7-38-25-11, 37-4-12

29-15-21-28-18-10-7 26-7 7-31 34-22-9-28-1-24-13-20-36;

29-28-7 2-8 6-28-7 2-38-3 24-15-36-21-28-15 32-25

2-38-16 7-11-4-7.

R
D
O
E
B
W
A
H
T

CLUES

Used in archery (2 Samuel 22:35): B ____ ____

Another name for Jesus (John 1:1): ____ ____ ____ ____

The payment for sin (Romans 6:23):

____ ____ ____ ____ ____

WORD SEARCH

THE SUN'S RACETRACK

Their **line** has gone out through all the earth, and their words to the end of the **world**. In them He has set a **tabernacle** for the **sun**, which is like a **bridegroom** coming out of his **chamber**, and **rejoices** as a **strong man** to run a **race**. Its going forth is from the **end** of the heaven, and its **circuit** to the ends of it, and there is **nothing hidden** from its heat.

PSALM 19:4–6 SKJV

SPOTTY HEADLINE

JO●HUA LEAVES ●WELVE ●BJECT● FOR REM●MBRA●CE

Hint: They came straight from the river.

___ ___ ___ ___ ___ ___

T	S	E	C	I	O	J	E	R	G
Z	Y	R	J	D	R	C	N	N	L
K	V	V	L	A	I	P	I	E	C
F	D	R	C	R	S	H	L	D	H
N	O	E	C	D	T	U	L	D	A
W	G	U	W	O	N	P	N	I	M
C	I	N	N	P	Q	E	M	H	B
T	A	B	E	R	N	A	C	L	E
S	T	R	O	N	G	M	A	N	R
B	R	I	D	E	G	R	O	O	M

RAiN

Across

2. "He gives rain on the __________ and sends water on the fields" (Job 5:10 NLV)
4. "And the __________ was forty days upon the earth" (Genesis 7:17 KJV)
7. "And he __________ again, and the heaven gave rain" (James 5:18 KJV)
8. God "sendeth rain on the just and on the __________" (Matthew 5:45 KJV)

Down

1. "I will give you rain in due __________" (Leviticus 26:4 KJV)
3. God "gave us rain from __________" (Acts 14:17 KJV)
5. "My doctrine shall __________ as the rain" (Deuteronomy 32:2 KJV)
6. "May He come down like rain upon the cut __________" (Psalm 72:6 NLV)

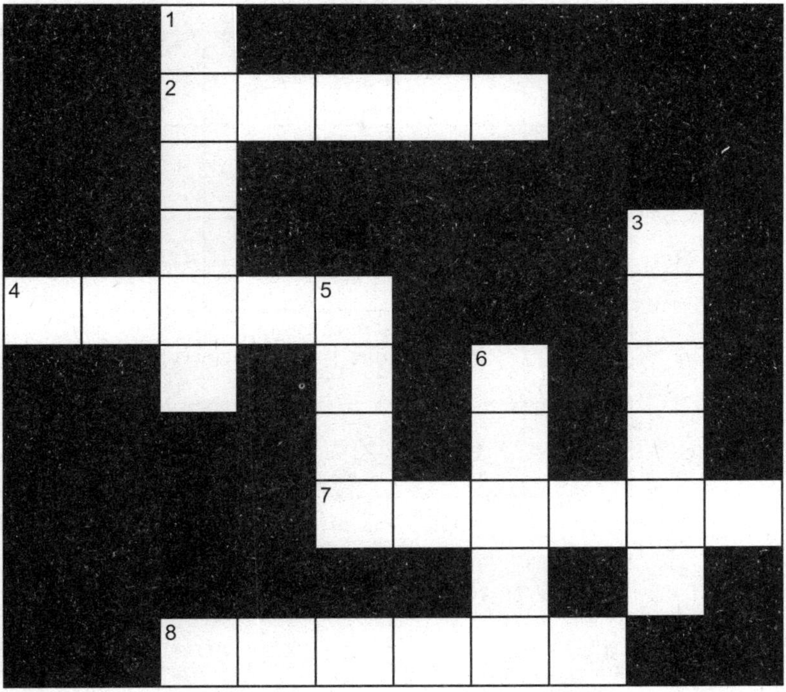
1
2
3
4
5
6
7
8

SCRAMBLED PLACE

WADE IN DANCING

Hint: Where Jesus' first miracle happened.

___ ___ ___ ___ ___ ___ ___

___ ___   ___ ___ ___ ___

DECODER

	1	2	3	4	5
1	C	Y	T	I	L
2	W	K	O	G	X
3	P	B	J	A	D
4	R	S	H	V	N
5	M	E	Z	U	F

James 1:2 NLV

51-12 11-43-41-14-42-13-14-34-45 32-41-23-13-43-52-41-42,

12-23-54 42-43-23-54-15-35 32-52 43-34-31-31-12

21-43-52-45 12-23-54 43-34-44-52 34-15-15

22-14-45-35-42 23-55 13-52-42-13-42.

The Great Flood

GENESIS 6:8 KJV

Because humanity had become so evil, God sent a great flood to destroy them. . .all except one person and his family. Crack the code to find out who that person was.

"There were _________ in the earth in those days" (6:4 KJV, SKJV) 18-9-7-12-15-26

"Then the Lord saw that man was very _________ on the earth" (6:5 NLV) 21-5-27-22-1-3

So the Lord said, "I will _________ man whom I have made" (6:7 NLV) 23-17-14-13-28-4-25

"All in whose nostrils was the _________ of life. . .died" (7:22 KJV) 29-6-24-2-30-20

"He took of every _________ animal" (8:20 NLV) 19-8-16-10-11

29-1-15 12-4-10-20 22-4-1-11-23 18-28-7-19-17 9-27

30-20-17 24-25-16-14 4-22 13-20-16 3-4-6-23.

Following Instructions

And his **servants** came near and spoke to him and said, "**My father**, if the prophet had told you to do some **great** thing, **would** you not have done it? How much **more**, then, when he says to you, '**Wash** and be **clean**'?" Then he **went** down and **dipped** himself **seven** times in the **Jordan**, according to the word of the **man of God**, and his **skin** was **restored** like the skin of a little child, and he was clean.

2 Kings 5:13–14 SKJV

SPOTTY HEADLINE

JE●●S D●AMA●●C●LLY
SHI●●S APPE●●●●●CE
WH●LE GL●WI●●

Hint: A long word that means "change."

___ ___ ___ ___ ___ ___ ___ ___ ___

___ ___ ___ ___ ___ ___ ___

G	R	E	A	T	S	K	I	N	V
Y	S	D	E	R	O	T	S	E	R
D	T	O	M	K	W	N	N	E	X
E	N	G	O	P	M	O	H	E	N
P	A	F	R	P	C	T	U	E	W
P	V	O	E	W	A	W	V	L	K
I	R	N	N	F	A	E	Q	K	D
D	E	A	Y	S	S	Q	L	R	F
T	S	M	H	N	A	E	L	C	T
J	O	R	D	A	N	N	T	G	X

CROSSWORD

Fire

Across

3. "His word was in mine heart as a burning fire shut up in my _________" (Jeremiah 20:9 KJV)
5. God spoke to Moses through a burning _________ (Exodus 3:2)
7. "Think it not strange concerning the fiery _________ which is to try you" (1 Peter 4:12 KJV)
8. God "makes His angels spirits, His ministers a _________ fire" (Psalm 104:4 SKJV)
9. "Every man's _________ shall be. . .revealed by fire" (1 Corinthians 3:13 KJV)

Down

1. "He shall baptize you with the Holy _________ and with fire" (Matthew 3:11 SKJV)
2. "For our God is a _________ fire" (Hebrews 12:29 KJV)
4. "And Mount Sinai was altogether covered with ________" (Exodus 19:18 SKJV)
6. "And the LORD went before them. . .by night in a _________ of fire" (Exodus 13:21 KJV)

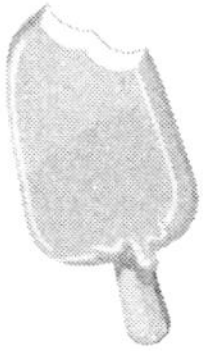

1
2
3
4
5
6
7
8
9

SPOTTY HEADLINE

E●●JAH ●HISKE● UP ●N
FIE●Y ●EATHER P●ENOME●ON

Hint: You might call it a tornado.

___ ___ ___ ___ ___ ___ ___ ___ ___

WORD SEARCH

FRAGILE AS GRASS

The **voice** said, "**Cry out**." And he said, "**What** shall I cry?" "All flesh is **grass**, and all its **loveliness** is like the **flower** of the **field**. The grass **withers**, the flower **fades**, because the **breath** of the LORD blows on it. **Surely** the people are grass. The grass withers, the flower fades, but the **word** of **our God** shall stand **forever**."

ISAIAH 40:6–8 SKJV

SPOTTY HEADLINE

UNT●L● AM●UNT● ●F ●EAVY R●I● KEEPS ●AL●ING

Hint: It took an ark to escape.

____ ____ ____ ____ ' ____

____ ____ ____ ____ ____

L	O	V	E	L	I	N	E	S	S
Y	U	F	N	H	G	R	S	T	Y
L	R	G	W	R	T	R	D	W	F
E	G	W	L	U	E	A	A	I	G
R	O	P	O	H	G	F	E	S	L
U	D	Y	T	R	J	L	C	R	S
S	R	I	B	M	D	O	I	R	B
C	W	W	H	A	T	W	O	N	T
K	S	E	D	A	F	E	V	R	M
F	O	R	E	V	E	R	T	X	Z

BIBLE DIAMOND

L
A
O
U
B
N
G
E
H

CLUES

Found in your body (Genesis 2:23): B ___ ___ ___

Mountain of curses (Deuteronomy 11:29):

___ ___ ___ ___

What you do when something's funny (Genesis 21:6):

___ ___ ___ ___ ___

Samson's Oddest Battle

Judges 15:15 SKJV

Samson was far from perfect, but God gave him amazing strength to defeat Israel's enemies. Crack the code to read about one of his strangest (and most impressive) victories.

The Israelites had been captive for ________ years (13:1)	22-32-17-30-27
Samson's father (13:2)	28-33-29-4-9-8
"Then the Philistines. . .camped in ________" (15:9 SKJV)	25-19-35-20-23
"And they bound him with two new ________ " (15:13 KJV)	2-12-34-16-3
"Now tell me, I ask, with what you might be ________" (16:10 SKJV)	11-6-14-5-36
"If they bind me tightly with new ropes. . . then I shall be ________" (16:11 SKJV)	26-31-7-1
Questioned Samson about his power (16:6, 10, 15–16)	21-37-15-10-18-24-13

33-5-35 8-37 22-4-14-29-16 9 29-37-26

25-33-26-11-32-5-31 12-22 24 36-6-5-1-37-27 24-5-21

3-30-17-37-30-2-23-31-35 12-19-30 13-10-3 8-9-5-36

9-29-35 30-32-6-1 10-30 24-29-16 3-18-37-26 7

30-13-4-14-3-7-5-21 28-37-29 26-10-30-23 10-30.

night

Across

2. Betrayed Jesus at night (John 13:29–30)

6. "The night cometh, when no man can ________" (John 9:4 KJV)

7. "The day of the Lord so cometh as a ________ in the night" (1 Thessalonians 5:2 KJV)

9. Jesus "continued all night in ________ to God" (Luke 6:12 KJV)

Down

1. "Those who get ________ do it at night" (1 Thessalonians 5:7 NLV)

3. "If a man walks in the night, he ________ because there is no light in him" (John 11:10 SKJV)

4. "Therefore let us not sleep. . .but let us watch and be ________" (1 Thessalonians 5:6 KJV)

5. "And in the fourth ________ of the night Jesus went unto them" (Matthew 14:25 KJV)

8. "The night is far spent, the ________ is at hand" (Romans 13:12 KJV)

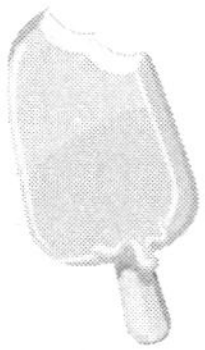

1
2
3
4
5
6
7
8
9

SPOTTY HEADLINE

●ESUS B●PTIZE● I●
FAM●US ●IVER

Hint: The name of a modern country.

___ ___ ___ ___ ___ ___

Beautiful Nature

The trees of the LORD are full of **sap**, the **cedars** of **Lebanon**, which He has **planted**, where the birds **make** their **nests**. As for the **stork**, the **fir** trees are her **house**. The **high hills** are a refuge for the wild **goats**, and the **rocks** for the **hyrax**.

PSALM 104:16–18 SKJV

SPOTTY HEADLINE

FRIG●T●NI●G CRE●●URE
DESCR●BED IN VI●ID DET●I●

Hint: You can read about it in the book of Job.

___ ___ ___ ___ ___ ___ ___ ___ ___

G	R	L	E	B	A	N	O	N	K
E	L	P	K	G	Y	R	T	B	S
S	R	M	L	K	O	M	I	R	N
U	O	K	L	A	N	A	A	F	M
O	C	N	H	E	N	D	T	C	A
H	K	L	S	Y	E	T	X	S	K
R	S	T	H	C	R	P	E	C	E
J	S	G	H	P	P	A	W	D	B
P	I	K	R	O	T	S	X	W	R
H	H	I	L	L	S	M	D	J	L

DECODER

	1	2	3	4	5
1	F	O	W	U	P
2	E	G	L	I	T
3	A	D	Z	K	S
4	V	N	C	B	X
5	R	Y	J	M	H

1 John 4:8 NLV

25-55-12-35-21 13-55-12 32-12 42-12-25 23-12-41-21 32-12

42-12-25 34-42-12-13 22-12-32 44-21-43-31-14-35-21

22-12-32 24-35 23-12-41-21.

BIBLE DIAMOND

A
E
T
N
S
L
O
O
M

CLUES

Wisest king (1 Kings 4:29):

S ____ ____ ____ ____ ____ ____

Found on your face (Job 41:2): ____ ____ ____ ____

What you do at dinner (Genesis 2:17): ____ ____ ____

"FAIR" WEATHER

"You have heard that it has been said, 'You shall **love** your **neighbor** and **hate** your enemy.' But I say to you, love your enemies, **bless** those who **curse** you, do **good** to those who hate you, and **pray** for those who despitefully use you and **persecute** you, that you may be the **children** of your **Father** who is in heaven. For He makes His sun to rise on **the evil** and on the good, and **sends** rain on the **just** and on the **unjust**."

MATTHEW 5:43–45 SKJV

SPOTTY HEADLINE

●ECKL●SS A●OSTLE
CU●S OFF AN ●AR

Hint: He was trying to protect Jesus from arrest.

___ ___ ___ ___ ___

E	L	N	E	R	D	L	I	H	C
T	H	A	T	E	N	Z	P	U	G
U	L	R	X	F	S	B	N	O	R
C	B	C	E	D	Q	J	O	O	T
E	Y	L	N	H	U	D	B	C	H
S	Z	E	E	S	T	H	D	U	E
R	S	V	T	S	G	A	T	R	E
E	C	O	X	I	S	T	F	S	V
P	Q	L	E	Y	A	R	P	E	I
Q	M	N	F	P	J	U	S	T	L

The Resurrection

John 20:28 NLV

When Jesus rose from the dead, not everyone believed right away—including Thomas. Crack the code to read Thomas' reaction when he found out the truth.

"But ________ stood without at the sepulchre weeping" (20:11 KJV)	25-4-6-12
"She thought He was the man who cared for the ________" (20:15 NLV)	18-17-21-23-15-9
"Jesus came and ________ among them" (20:19 NLV)	13-24-14-16-20
"Receive the ________ Spirit" (20:22 SKJV)	22-5-10-1
"Reach ________ thy finger" (20:27 KJV)	7-3-19-8-11-2

24-22-14-25-17-13 13-4-3-23 19-16 22-3-25, "25-1

10-14-2-20 17-9-20 25-12 18-5-20!"

DECODER

	1	2	3	4	5
1	W	T	U	D	P
2	Z	E	R	Y	K
3	A	N	I	B	F
4	X	S	V	G	L
5	J	O	M	C	H

MARK 11:10 KJV

34-45-22-42-42-22-14 34-22 12-55-22

25-33-32-44-14-52-53 52-35 52-13-23 35-31-12-55-22-23

14-31-43-33-14, 12-55-31-12 54-52-53-22-12-55 33-32

12-55-22 32-31-53-22 52-35 12-55-22 45-52-23-14:

55-52-42-31-32-32-31 33-32 12-55-22 55-33-44-55-22-42-12.

Clouds

Across

1. "He makes the clouds His wagon. He rides on the _________ of the wind" (Psalm 104:3 NLV)

2. "We which are alive. . .shall be _________ up together. . .in the clouds" (1 Thessalonians 4:17 KJV)

4. "He shall come up like the clouds, and his _________ shall be like a whirlwind" (Jeremiah 4:13 SKJV)

7. "He comes with clouds, and every _________ shall see Him" (Revelation 1:7 SKJV)

8. "The cloud covered the meeting _________" (Numbers 9:15 NLV)

Down

1. "He bindeth up the _________ in his thick clouds" (Job 26:8 KJV)

3. "He _________ the heavens with clouds" (Psalm 147:8 NLV)

5. "Hereafter shall ye see the Son of man. . .coming in the clouds of _________" (Matthew 26:64 KJV)

6. "The clouds are the _________ of [God's] feet" (Nahum 1:3 KJV)

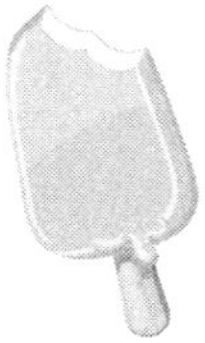

1
2
3
4
5
6
7
8

SCRAMBLED THING

WE MEANT TENTS

Hint: The part of the Bible where Jesus shows up.

___ ___ ___

___ ___ ___ ___ ___ ___ ___ ___ ___

SIMON, THE MAGIC MAN

But there was a **certain** man called **Simon**, who in the same city **formerly** used **sorcery** and **bewitched** the people of **Samaria**, saying that he was some **great one**, to whom they all paid **attention**, from the **least** to the **greatest**, saying, "This man is the great **power** of God." And they gave **regard** to him because for a long **time** he had bewitched them with sorceries.

ACTS 8:9–11 SKJV

SPOTTY HEADLINE

JOHN ●ECE●VES A ●ISIO●
OF ●H● ●POCO●YPS●

Hint: It's the last book of the Bible!

___ ___ ___ ___ ___ ___ ___ ___ ___ ___

D	E	H	C	T	I	W	E	B	N
E	F	O	R	M	E	R	L	Y	O
N	T	L	M	N	N	K	L	Z	I
O	S	T	S	I	E	Q	D	N	T
T	E	R	O	A	P	M	P	D	N
A	T	E	R	T	M	O	I	O	E
E	A	G	C	R	W	A	M	T	T
R	E	A	E	E	X	I	R	P	T
G	R	R	R	C	S	C	W	I	A
R	G	D	Y	L	E	A	S	T	A

God's Word

Across

3. "The words that I speak unto you, they are spirit, and they are ________" (John 6:63 KJV)

5. "All ________ is given by inspiration of God" (2 Timothy 3:16 SKJV)

7. "Be ye ________ of the word, and not hearers only" (James 1:22 KJV)

9. "Thy word have I ________ in mine heart, that I might not sin against thee" (Psalm 119:11 KJV)

10. "The Word was with God, and the Word ________ God" (John 1:1 KJV)

Down

1. "Blessed are they that hear the word of God, and ________ it" (Luke 11:28 KJV)

2. "How can a young man keep his way ________? By living by Your Word" (Psalm 119:9 NLV)

4. "Make them holy for Yourself by the truth. Your Word is ________" (John 17:17 NLV)

6. "Now ye are ________ through the word which I have spoken unto you" (John 15:3 KJV)

8. "For the word of God is. . .sharper than any twoedged ________" (Hebrews 4:12 KJV)

1
2
3
4
5
6
7
8
9
10

SPOTTY HEADLINE

GO● MAKES E●TREMELY
●E●VY OBJ●CT FLO●T

Hint: A miracle of Elisha.

___ ___ ___ ___ ___ ___

WEATHER PATTERNS

And He also said to the people, "When you **see** a cloud **rise** out of the **west**, immediately you say, 'There **comes** a **shower**.' And so it is. And when you see the **<u>south wind</u> blow**, you say, 'There will be **heat**.' And it comes **<u>to pass</u>**. You **hypocrites**! You can **discern** the face of the **sky** and of the earth, but how is it that you do not discern **<u>this time</u>**?"

LUKE 12:54–56 SKJV

SPOTTY HEADLINE

GO● M●KES LIG●●S IN THE SK● ●OR VA●IO●S SEAS●NS

Hint: Right in the middle of creation week.

___ ___ ___ ___ ___ ___   ___ ___ ___

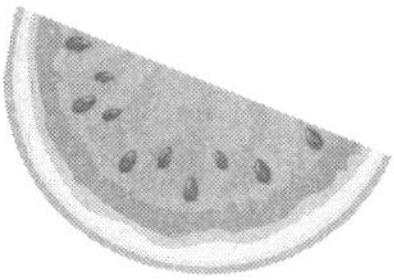

N	N	V	E	W	E	S	T	S	K
K	G	S	B	B	Y	W	J	H	P
M	I	L	S	K	M	Y	K	O	K
R	O	G	S	A	C	L	K	W	N
W	R	Q	K	K	P	O	Y	E	R
T	A	E	H	M	R	O	M	R	E
E	M	I	T	S	I	H	T	E	C
H	Y	P	O	C	R	I	T	E	S
R	V	M	B	H	Z	W	M	S	I
M	S	O	U	T	H	W	I	N	D

I
O
L
N
E
N
G
O
L

CLUES

He had a disgusting death (Judges 3:17, 21–22):

E ___ ___ ___ ___

Another word for Christmas: ___ ___ ___ ___

Animal killed by Samson (Judges 14:5–6):

___ ___ ___ ___

ACROSTIC

PAUL IN ATHENS

ACTS 17:32 KJV

When Paul came to Athens preaching the resurrection, it was unlike anything the people there had heard before. Crack the code to find out their reaction.

Greek philosophers who valued wisdom over pleasure (17:18 SKJV)	25-27-28-9-18-20
"He preaches about _________ gods" (17:18 NLV)	3-13-26-1-23-21-29
"God. . .made the _________ and all things therein" (17:24 KJV)	12-17-24-19-11
God "has made from one blood all nations of _________" (17:26 SKJV)	10-14-7
God "is not _________ from every one of us" (17:27 SKJV)	15-5-8
"We should not _________ of [God] as being like gold" (17:29 NLV)	4-16-6-22-2

25-17-10-29 10-28-18-2-14-11: 5-22-11 17-13-16-29-8-20

3-1-6-11, 12-29 12-9-19-19 6-14-5-26 4-16-29-14 1-21-5-9-7

17-15 13-16-6-3 10-5-4-27-29-8.

God's Amazing Creation

Across

1. "He sendeth the springs into the ________" (Psalm 104:10 KJV)

6. "Thou coveredst it with the deep as with a ________" (Psalm 104:6 KJV)

7. "[God] laid the foundations of the ________" (Psalm 104:5 KJV)

8. "He touches the mountains and they ________" (Psalm 104:32 NLV)

9. "The trees of the LORD are full of ________" (Psalm 104:16 KJV)

Down

2. "He covers Himself with ________ as with a coat" (Psalm 104:2 NLV)

3. "When You [God] take away their breath, they die and ________ to the dust" (Psalm 104:29 NLV)

4. "There is that ________, whom You have made to play in [the sea]" (Psalm 104:26 SKJV)

5. "The high mountains are for the wild ________" (Psalm 104:18 NLV)

1
2
3
4
5
6
7
8
9

SPOTTY HEADLINE

K●NG BEGIN● REIGN AT
●UST EIG●T YE●RS ●F AGE

Hint: He was one of the good ones.

___ ___ ___ ___ ___ ___

WINDY DEPARTURE

When they had **crossed**, **Elijah** said to **Elisha**, "Ask what I should do for you before I am **taken** from you." And Elisha said, "I ask you, let **twice** the share of your **spirit** be **upon me**." Elijah said, "You have asked a **hard** thing. But if you see me when I am taken from you, it will be given to you. But if not, it will not be so." As they went on and **talked**, a war-**wagon** of **fire** and **horses** of fire came between them. And Elijah **went up** by a **windstorm** to heaven.

2 KINGS 2:9–11 NLV

SCRAMBLED EVENT

ONE IS A RAG

Hint: Jesus' third-day miracle

___ ___ ___ ___   ___ ___ ___ ___ ___

C	M	W	A	G	O	N	R	M	M
B	R	D	D	S	E	S	R	O	H
T	O	E	E	E	L	I	S	H	A
T	T	S	K	E	M	N	O	P	U
W	S	S	L	T	M	Q	S	K	H
I	D	O	A	W	A	P	K	A	L
C	N	R	T	R	I	K	J	V	E
E	I	C	A	R	Z	I	E	R	N
Z	W	K	I	H	L	G	I	N	Z
P	U	T	N	E	W	F	Y	X	L

ANIMALS

Across

1. "Who gets the food ready for the raven, when its young __________ to God?" (Job 38:41 NLV)

4. "The __________ of you. . .shall be on every beast of the earth" (Genesis 9:2 SKJV)

5. "The wolf and the __________ will eat together" (Isaiah 65:25 NLV)

8. "Are not two __________ sold for a farthing?" (Matthew 10:29 KJV)

Down

1. "And God said, Let the earth bring forth the living __________ after his kind" (Genesis 1:24 KJV)

2. "A righteous man regardeth the __________ of his beast" (Proverbs 12:10 KJV)

3. "And God created great __________, and every living creature that moveth" (Genesis 1:21 KJV)

6. "He giveth to the __________ his food" (Psalm 147:9 KJV)

7. "Even the __________ in the sky knows her times" (Jeremiah 8:7 NLV)

9. "You shall not __________ with an ox and a donkey together" (Deuteronomy 23:10 SKJV)

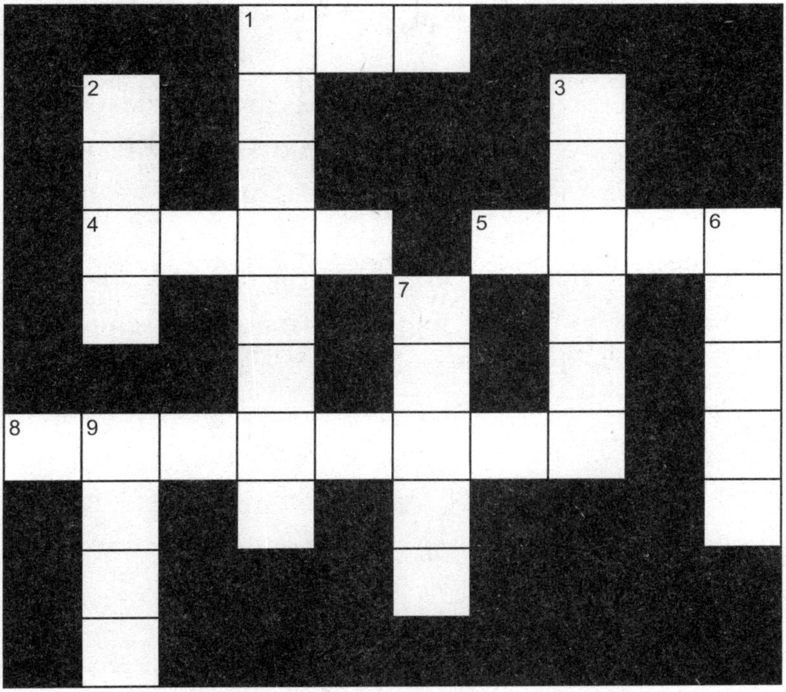
1
2
3
4
5
6
7
8
9

SPOTTY HEADLINE

GOD P●CK● N●TION
FO● HIMS●●F

Hint: There's still a nation by this name!

___ ___ ___ ___ ___ ___

WORD SEARCH

UNSETTLING MESSAGE

Then they brought the golden **vessels** that were taken out of the temple of the **house of God** that was in **Jerusalem**. And the king and his **princes**, his wives and his concubines drank out of them. They drank **wine** and praised the gods of gold and **silver**, of **bronze**, of **iron**, of **wood**, and of stone. In the same hour, **fingers** of a man's hand **emerged** and wrote opposite the candlestick on the **plaster** of the wall of the king's palace. And the king saw the part of the hand that wrote. Then the king's face was changed and his thoughts **troubled** him, so that the joints of his loins were loosed and his knees knocked against one another.

DANIEL 5:3–6 SKJV

SPOTTY HEADLINE

J●●US SEN●S T●OUSA●DS O● ●VIL SPI●ITS INTO UN●ITT●NG H●STS

Hint: They met a watery end.

___ ___ ___ ___   ___ ___

___ ___ ___ ___ ___

L	F	I	N	G	E	R	S	C	D
P	D	Z	K	Z	W	I	T	O	P
R	E	E	S	N	L	I	G	G	L
I	G	F	L	V	O	F	N	Z	A
N	R	L	E	B	O	R	V	E	S
C	E	R	S	E	U	D	I	V	T
E	M	N	S	F	T	O	J	N	E
S	E	U	E	Z	N	O	R	B	R
V	O	C	V	M	K	W	W	T	F
H	J	E	R	U	S	A	L	E	M

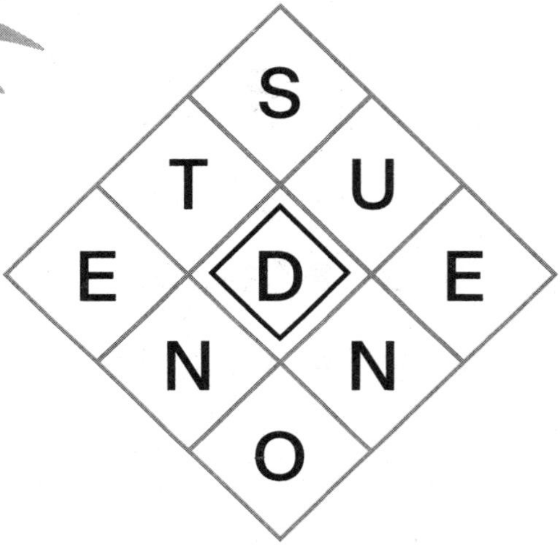
S
T
U
E
D
E
N
N
O

CLUES

What God used to make man (Genesis 2:7):

D ___ ___ ___

Number of main commandments (Exodus 34:28):

___ ___ ___

How many are righteous, besides God (Psalm 14:3 KJV):

___ ___ ___ ___

Daniel in the Lions' Den

Daniel 6:22 KJV

Some wicked men convinced the king to sign a law against praying to God. But Daniel didn't follow that rule, so he was tossed into a den of lions. Crack the code to find out what happened.

"King ________, live forever!" (6:6 NLV)
9-26-12-6-10-21

"[We] have consulted together to establish a ________ statute" (6:7 KJV)
22-16-8-19-7

"So King Darius made the law and wrote his ________ on it" (6:9 NLV)
20-11-18-25

"Then the king went to his palace, and passed the ________ fasting" (6:18 KJV)
17-3-24-14-15

"Daniel, ________ of the living God" (6:20 NLV)
27-23-2-4-13-1-5

18-8 24-16-9 14-26-15-14 21-25-17-5 14-6-27

19-20-24-23-7, 11-1-9 14-13-5-14 21-14-10-5 15-14-25

7-3-16-1-21' 18-16-10-15-14-21, 15-14-11-15 5-14-25-8

14-26-4-23 17-16-15 14-10-2-5 18-25.

CROSSWORD

The Fall of Jericho

Across

2. "She. . .hid them with the __________ of flax" (Joshua 2:6 KJV)

4. Joshua's father (Joshua 2:1)

5. "And they utterly __________ all that was in the city" (Joshua 6:21 KJV)

8. "Let seven __________ bear seven trumpets" (Joshua 6:6 KJV)

Down

1. " __________ is the man. . .who. . .builds this city Jericho" (Joshua 6:26 SKJV)

3. "Thou shalt bind this line of __________ thread in the window" (Joshua 2:18 KJV)

6. On the seventh day, the Israelites circled Jericho __________ times (Joshua 6:15–16)

7. "The __________ of the covenant of the LORD followed them" (Joshua 6:8 KJV)

9. "Have all the men of war go around the city once. Do this for __________ days" (Joshua 6:3 NLV)

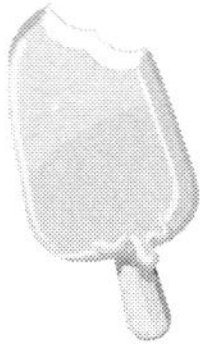

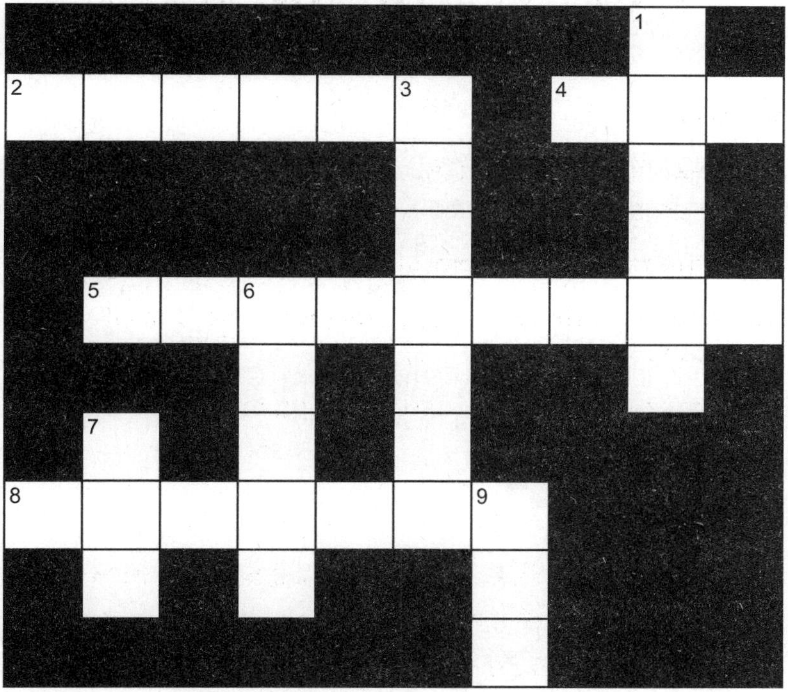
1
2
3
4
5
6
7
8
9

SPOTTY HEADLINE

●ON OF GO● ●●●KS OUT TW●LVE UNL●KELY FOL●OWER●

Hint: They learned from Jesus for three years, then built the church.

___ ___ ___ ___ ___ ___ ___ ___ ___

Job's Response to Tragedy

Then Job **arose** and **tore** his **robe** and **shaved** his **head** and **fell down** on the ground and **worshipped** and said, "**Naked** I came out of my mother's **womb** and naked I shall **return** there. The LORD **gave** and the Lord has **taken** away. **Blessed** be the name of the LORD." In all this Job did not sin or charge God **foolishly**.

JOB 1:20–22 SKJV

SPOTTY HEADLINE

ONE OF ●ES●S' ●EAR FRIEND● BETR●YS HIM

Hint: He was also known as Iscariot.

___ ___ ___ ___ ___

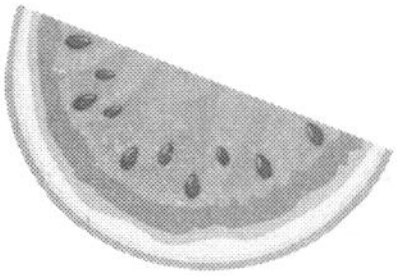

Y	L	H	S	I	L	O	O	F	W
W	M	N	R	U	T	E	R	J	O
B	L	E	S	S	E	D	N	D	R
B	M	O	W	G	F	W	R	L	S
S	F	Y	E	R	O	B	E	E	H
T	H	R	T	D	Y	N	N	S	I
N	O	A	L	W	E	A	H	O	P
T	Z	L	V	K	K	V	E	R	P
K	E	M	A	E	B	M	A	A	E
F	J	T	D	J	D	F	D	G	D

CROSSWORD

ELIJAH LEAVES-ELISHA STEPS IN

Across

1. Elisha "took hold of his own ________, and rent them in two pieces" (2 Kings 2:12 KJV)

4. "And ________ men of the sons of the prophets went, and stood to view afar off" (2 Kings 2:7 KJV)

5. Elijah went up in a ________ (2 Kings 2:11)

7. Elisha "took the ________ of Elijah that fell from him, and smote the waters" (2 Kings 2:14 KJV)

8. "There appeared a chariot of fire, and ________ of fire" (2 Kings 2:11 KJV)

Down

2. "The ________ of Elijah doth rest on Elisha" (2 Kings 2:15 KJV)

3. "Remain here, I ask, for the LORD has sent me to the ________" (2 Kings 2:6 SKJV)

6. "I pray thee, let a ________ portion of thy spirit be upon me" (2 Kings 2:9 KJV)

SPOTTY HEADLINE

GOD P●RFO●●S
IMPOS●●B●E ●●TIONS

Hint: Also called "signs" and "wonders."

___ ___ ___ ___ ___ ___ ___ ___

Under the Fig Tree

Jesus saw **Nathanael** coming to Him and said, "**See**! There is a **true** Jew. There is **nothing** false in him." Nathanael said to Jesus, "How do **You know** me?" Jesus **answered** him, "Before **Philip** talked to you, I saw you **under** the fig tree." Nathanael said to Him, "**Teacher**, You are the **Son of God**. You are the **King** of the **Jews**."

JOHN 1:47–49 NLV

SPOTTY HEADLINE

●ALKING A●IMAL DECO●IVE●
INNOC●NT ●E●SON

Hint: Another name for a snake.

___ ___ ___ ___ ___ ___ ___

S	D	S	W	E	J	K	A	L	R
O	F	S	E	E	G	N	E	N	E
N	L	W	D	N	S	A	P	O	H
O	W	R	I	W	N	W	S	T	C
F	T	K	E	A	W	M	U	H	A
G	Q	R	H	D	N	M	S	I	E
O	E	T	U	J	N	K	E	N	T
D	A	N	C	E	F	U	J	G	C
N	Z	N	P	I	L	I	H	P	T
B	Y	O	U	K	N	O	W	X	L

O
L
O
L
P
S
I
E
V

CLUES

A very small body of water (John 5:2): P ____ ____ ____

Untie; allow to go free (Matthew 16:19 KJV, SKJV):

____ ____ ____ ____ ____

Bad; wicked (Mark 3:4 SKJV): ____ ____ ____ ____

God Calls Samuel

1 SAMUEL 3:7 KJV

When God called little Samuel in the dead of night, the boy didn't know what was going on. Crack the code to find out why.

"And the child Samuel ________ unto the LORD before Eli" (3:1 KJV) 19-16-1-11-27-25-6-10-12-30

"Samuel was ________ down to sleep" (3:3 KJV) 15-34-26-8

"Speak, LORD, ________ your servant hears" (3:9 SKJV) 13-9-17

"The ears of ________ who hears it shall tingle" (3:11 SKJV) 3-22-21-18-7-20-29-4

"I will judge his ________ forever" (3:13 SKJV) 32-24-5-2-23

"And all Israel. . .________ that Samuel was. . .a prophet" (3:20 SKJV) 28-14-33-31

1-9-31 27-34-19-2-6-15 30-16-8 29-20-25 7-12-25

28-14-24-31 25-32-3 15-9-10-8, 14-21-26-25-32-4-17

31-34-2 25-32-23 31-9-18-30 24-13 25-32-33 15-9-17-8

7-12-25 18-23-22-6-34-15-3-30 5-1-25-9 32-11-19.

CROSSWORD

STORMS

Across

4. "A wind storm came over the _________" (Luke 8:23 NLV)

6. "Master, master, we _________ " (Luke 8:24 KJV)

8. "A bad storm came over the lake. The waves were covering the _________ " (Matthew 8:24 NLV)

9. "He maketh the storm a calm, so that the _________ thereof are still" (Psalm 107:29 KJV)

Down

1. Jesus "said unto the sea, _________, be still" (Mark 4:39 KJV)

2. "There was a mighty _________ in the sea" (Jonah 1:4 KJV)

3. "Thou rulest the _________ of the sea" (Psalm 89:9 KJV)

5. And there shall be a. . .place of refuge and a _________ from storm and from rain" (Isaiah 4:6 SKJV)

7. "It is the _________ Who makes the storm clouds" (Zechariah 10:1 NLV)

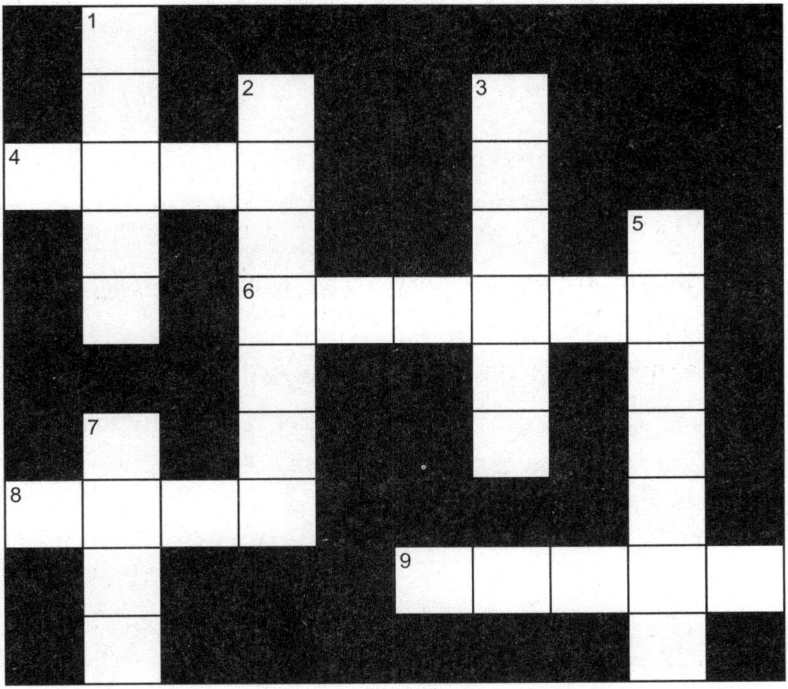
1
2
3
4
5
6
7
8
9

SCRAMBLED PERSONS

HUNTS FOR NODES

Hint: Nickname for James and John (Mark 3:17).

___ ___ ___ ___   ___ ___

___ ___ ___ ___ ___ ___ ___

A New Apostle Is Chosen

And they **appointed two**: **Joseph** called Barsabbas, who was surnamed **Justus**, and **Matthias**. And they **prayed** and said, "You, Lord, who know the **hearts** of all men, show which of these two You have **chosen**, that he may take part in this **ministry** and apostleship from which **Judas** fell by transgression, that he might go to his own **place**." And they gave **forth** their **lots**, and the lot fell on Matthias. And he was numbered with the **eleven** apostles.

ACTS 1:23–26 SKJV

SPOTTY HEADLINE

GID●ON R●QU●STS CON●IRMATION WITH UNUSUA● OBJE●T

Hint: He was too sheepish to begin without knowing for sure.

___ ___ ___ ___ ___ ___

S	D	R	C	J	O	S	E	P	H
A	E	Y	P	R	A	Y	E	D	E
D	T	Y	R	H	X	L	K	M	L
U	N	X	T	T	T	C	H	A	E
J	I	R	J	O	S	E	X	T	V
Q	O	L	W	U	A	I	P	T	E
F	P	T	O	R	S	L	N	H	N
N	P	Y	T	T	A	T	F	I	L
H	A	S	C	C	S	V	U	A	M
W	Y	N	E	S	O	H	C	S	K

Crying

Across

3. "My face is _________ from crying, and darkness is over my eyes" (Job 16:16 NLV)

5. "Put thou my tears into thy _________ : are they not in thy book?" (Psalm 56:8 KJV)

7. "Mine eye runneth down with _________ of water" (Lamentations 3:48 KJV)

8. "Blessed are ye that weep now: for ye shall _________ " (Luke 6:21 KJV)

Down

1. "And when [Jesus] was come near, he beheld the _________ , and wept over it" (Luke 19:41 KJV)

2. "Those who plant with tears will gather fruit with songs of _________ " (Psalm 126:5 NLV)

3. "He that goes forth and weepeth. . .shall doubtless come again with _________ " (Psalm 126:6 KJV)

4. "For I have eaten _________ like bread, and mingled my drink with weeping" (Psalm 102:9 KJV)

6. "My eyes, my soul and my body are becoming _________ from being sad" (Psalm 31:9 NLV)

1
2
3
4
5
6
7
8

SPOTTY HEADLINE

●EAUT●F●L HEAVENLY ●REATU●ES ●AVE ●ANY ●YES

Hint: Special kinds of angels.

___ ___ ___ ___ ___ ___ ___ ___

WORD SEARCH

God's Unspeakable Power

"Who has **<u>cut open</u>** a way for the flood, and a **path** for the thunderstorm? Who **brings** rain on the land without people, on a **desert** without a man in it, to fill the **need** of the **<u>wasted land</u>**, and to make the grass grow? Does the rain have a father? Who has given **birth** to the **drops** of rain? Who gave birth to **ice**? And who gave birth to the **<u>snow water</u>** of heaven? Water becomes hard like **stone**, and the **top** of the sea is **covered** with ice."

JOB 38:25–30 NLV

SPOTTY HEADLINE

JOSE●● S●LD ●O MASTE●
●N L●ND OF EGY●T

Hint: The man's wife couldn't keep her eyes off Joseph.

___ ___ ___ ___ ___ ___ ___ ___

W	T	J	T	O	P	N	M	D	J
D	N	E	Q	G	L	E	M	N	S
N	E	L	C	E	N	E	B	A	N
J	P	S	N	I	H	D	M	L	O
Z	O	O	E	T	E	B	N	D	W
J	T	N	A	R	I	K	G	E	W
S	U	P	E	R	T	Q	M	T	A
T	C	V	T	J	Z	D	Q	S	T
L	O	H	S	P	O	R	D	A	E
C	M	B	R	I	N	G	S	W	R

S
H
I
A
F
R
L
S
T

CLUES

Swallowed Jonah (Jonah 1:17): F ___ ___ ___

One of two equal parts (Esther 7:2): ___ ___ ___ ___

Day on which light was made (Genesis 1:3–5):

___ ___ ___ ___ ___

DECODER

	1	2	3	4	5
1	O	G	I	S	K
2	L	E	Y	N	V
3	H	A	W	X	T
4	B	R	Z	U	P
5	M	F	J	D	C

Jonah 1:9 SKJV

32-24-54 31-22 14-32-13-54 35-11 35-31-22-51, "13 32-51 32 31-22-41-42-22-33, 32-24-54 13 52-22-32-42 35-31-22 21-11-42-54, 35-31-22 12-11-54 11-52 31-22-32-25-22-24, 33-31-11 31-32-14 51-32-54-22 35-31-22 14-22-32 32-24-54 35-31-22 54-42-23 21-32-24-54."

THE FALL

Across

1. "Who told thee that thou wast __________?" (Genesis 3:11 KJV)

4. "Because thou hast done this, thou art cursed above all __________" (Genesis 3:14 KJV)

6. "And I will put __________ between thee and the woman" (Genesis 3:15 KJV)

7. "Now the serpent was more __________ than any beast of the field" (Genesis 3:1 SKJV)

8. "And the serpent said unto the woman, Ye shall not surely __________ " (Genesis 3:4 KJV)

Down

2. "Upon thy belly shalt thou go, and dust shalt thou __________ all the days of thy life" (Genesis 3:14 KJV)

3. "And the woman said, The serpent __________ me, and I did eat" (Genesis 3:13 KJV)

4. God "placed __________ east of the garden of Eden with a sword of fire" (Genesis 3:24 NLV)

5. "Your eyes shall be opened, and ye shall be as __________" (Genesis 3:5 KJV)

1
2
3
4
5
6
7
8

SPOTTY HEADLINE

●TR●NG ●●N KILL● A LIO●

Hint: His long hair played a role.

___ ___ ___ ___ ___ ___

nice TRY. . .

Again the **devil** took Jesus to a very high **mountain**. He had Jesus **look** at all the nations of the world to see how great they were. He said to Jesus, "I will **give** You all these nations if You will get down at my feet and **worship** me." Jesus said to the devil, "**<u>Get away</u>**, **Satan**. It is **written**, 'You **must** worship the Lord your God. You must **obey** Him only.'" Then the devil **went** away from Jesus. **Angels** came and **cared** for Him.

MATTHEW 4:8–11 NLV

SPOTTY HEADLINE

MO●ES S●OCKED BY ●●RNING OBJECT

Hint: A shrub that never burned up.

___ ___ ___ ___

R	G	L	G	E	T	A	W	A	Y
G	R	G	O	L	B	P	Q	D	L
I	R	T	I	O	N	J	N	Q	T
V	B	V	S	X	K	L	I	S	A
E	E	M	O	U	N	T	A	I	N
D	Y	G	T	N	M	T	G	T	G
D	E	R	A	C	A	L	A	K	E
R	B	X	R	N	W	E	N	T	L
T	O	N	E	T	T	I	R	W	S
V	V	W	O	R	S	H	I	P	F

THE HOLY SPIRIT ARRIVES

ACTS 2:1 SKJV

Not long after Jesus ascended, the disciples were filled with the Holy Spirit. Crack the code to find out the setting for this amazing miracle.

"A sound. . .as of a rushing mighty _________"
(2:2 KJV) 14-20-16-4

"And there _________ unto them
cloven tongues like as of fire"
(2:3 KJV) 19-2-29-3-25-34-6-28

"But this is what was spoken by the
_________ Joel" (2:16 SKJV) 18-7-30-11-23-26-10

"By _________ and wonders and
signs" (2:22 SKJV) 8-33-36-31-27-21-37-24

"Neither wilt thou _________ thine Holy
One to see corruption" (2:27 KJV) 1-9-17-13-15-22

"And _________ wonders and signs were
done by the apostles" (2:43 KJV) 32-12-35-5

19-16-4 14-23-15-35 10-23-37 28-25-5 30-17

18-3-16-10-37-27-30-24-10 23-31-28 13-9-21-21-5

27-30-8-26, 10-23-37-5 14-3-7-15 31-21-21 14-33-10-23

30-35-37 12-27-27-30-7-28 20-16 30-35-26 11-21-12-27-37.

U
L
O
O
S
S
T
P
E

CLUES

Part of you that never dies (Matthew 10:28):

S ____ ____ ____

Ancient dice-roll (Matthew 27:35 KJV, SKJV):

____ ____ ____ ____

Led up to the altar (Exodus 20:26):

____ ____ ____ ____ ____

The Tower of Babel

Across

2. "And the LORD said, "Behold, the __________ are one" (Genesis 11:6 SKJV)

5. "This is only the __________ of what they will do" (Genesis 11:6 NLV)

6. "So the LORD scattered them abroad from thence upon the __________ of all the earth" (Genesis 11:8 KJV)

8. "And the LORD came down to see the __________ and the tower" (Genesis 11:5 KJV)

Down

1. "Come, __________ Us go down and there confound their language" (Genesis 11:7 SKJV)

3. "Now the whole earth used the same __________ and the same words" (Genesis 11:1 NLV)

4. "They found a valley in the land of __________ and made their home there" (Genesis 11:2 NLV)

5. "And they had __________ for stone" (Genesis 11:3 KJV)

7. "As they journeyed from the __________. . .they found a plain" (Genesis 11:2 KJV)

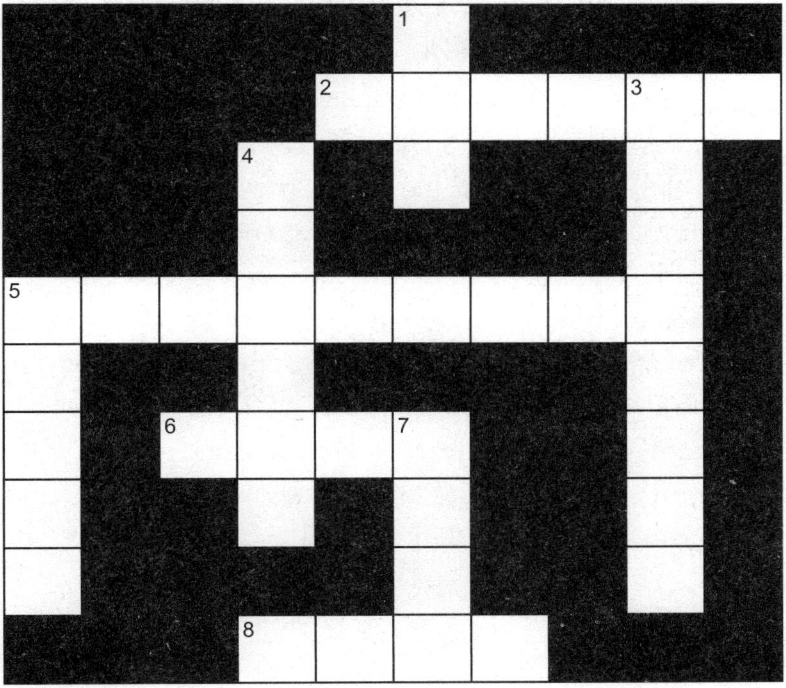
1
2
3
4
5
6
7
8

SPOTTY HEADLINE

JESUS C●EATES ●INE OU●
OF UNLIK●LY SUBST●NCE

Hint: It fills rivers, oceans, and storm clouds.

___ ___ ___ ___ ___

INTERESTING STRATEGY

And when he came to **Lehi**, the Philistines **shouted** against him. And the Spirit of the Lord came **mightily** on him, and the **cords** that were on his **arms** became as **flax** that was burned with fire, and his **bands loosed** from off his hands. And he found a new **jawbone** of a **donkey** and **stretched** out his hand and took it and **slew** a **thousand** men with it. And Samson said, "With the jawbone of a donkey, **heaps** on heaps, with the jaw of a donkey I have slain a thousand men."

JUDGES 15:14–16 SKJV

SCRAMBLED THING

MEN AT FIRM

Hint: Created to divide the waters.

___ ___ ___ ___ ___ ___ ___ ___ ___

H	E	A	P	S	Y	J	I	W	P
T	S	T	R	E	T	C	H	E	D
D	K	C	K	V	L	N	E	N	T
T	E	N	O	F	T	D	L	O	H
T	O	S	L	R	E	R	L	B	O
D	T	A	O	T	D	P	T	W	U
A	X	W	U	O	M	S	Q	A	S
R	H	O	L	S	L	E	W	J	A
M	H	K	S	D	N	A	B	M	N
S	M	I	G	H	T	I	L	Y	D

DECODER

	1	2	3	4	5
1	J	X	F	Y	I
2	T	A	M	D	S
3	N	U	E	R	O
4	W	B	L	C	Z
5	K	P	G	V	H

HEBREWS 3:4 KJV

13-35-34 33-54-33-34-14 55-35-32-25-33 15-25

42-32-15-43-24-33-24 42-14 25-35-23-33 23-22-31;

42-32-21 55-33 21-55-22-21 42-32-15-43-21

22-43-43 21-55-15-31-53-25 15-25 53-35-24.

Solomon's Fame

1 Kings 10:1 NLV

God gifted Solomon with incredible wisdom and riches, which drew the attention of a very powerful ruler. Crack the code to find out who it was.

"In Gibeon the LORD appeared to Solomon in a ________" (3:5 KJV) 4-12-20-1-6

Two women asked Solomon about a ________ who had died (3:19) 26-7-19-22-10

Famous for cedar trees (5:6) 16-18-29-28-2-5-11

"Hiram gave Solomon cedar trees and ________ trees" (5:10 KJV) 27-25-23

"I have surely built thee an house to ________ in" (8:13 KJV) 24-8-17-31-32

"And Solomon answered all her ________" (10:3 SKJV) 21-3-14-33-13-30-9-15-34

8-7-20-2 13-7-18 21-3-17-14-11 9-27 33-7-18-29-1

7-20-28-12-4 1-29-5-3-13 13-7-20 8-19-34-10-9-6

34-9-22-5-6-9-15 7-1-4 27-23-5-6 13-7-17 22-9-23-24,

33-7-14 26-1-6-18 13-5 13-20-34-13 7-25-6 8-30-13-7

7-1-23-4 21-3-20-34-13-25-5-2-33.

Oceans

Across

3. "When He set a _________ on the face of the depth. . ." (Proverbs 8:27 SKJV)

4. "All the rivers _________ into the sea; yet the sea is not full" (Ecclesiastes 1:7 KJV)

7. "Praise the LORD from the earth, ye _________, and all deeps" (Psalm 148:7 KJV)

9. "To him that stretched out the _________ above the waters. . ." (Psalm 136:6 KJV)

10. "So is this great and wide _________, wherein are things creeping innumerable" (Psalm 104:25 KJV)

Down

1. "He has surrounded the waters with _________" (Job 26:10 SKJV)

2. "Then I saw something that looked like a sea of _________ mixed with fire" (Revelation 15:2 NLV)

5. ". . .whatsoever passeth through the _________ of the seas" (Psalm 8:8 KJV)

6. "He makes the sea boil like a _________" (Job 41:31 NLV)

8. "And the sea gave up the _________ which were in it" (Revelation 20:13 KJV)

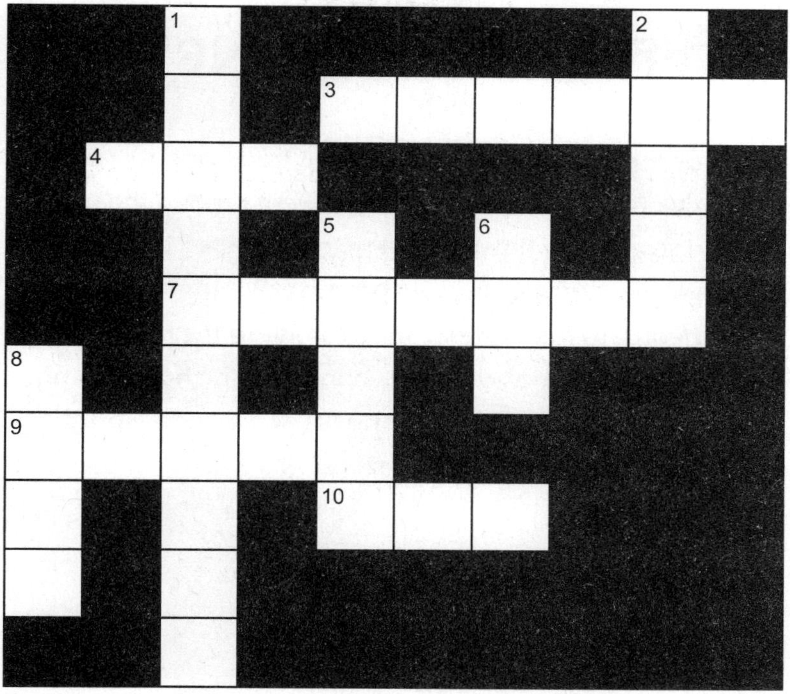
1
2
3
4
5
6
7
8
9
10

SPOTTY HEADLINE

DAVID WRITE● COL●ECTION OF ●ARVELOUS ●OEMS

Hint: You may've even memorized the 23rd.

___ ___ ___ ___ ___ ___

SWEET, FORBIDDEN HONEY

And all the **people** came among the **trees**, and there was **honey** on the ground. The people went among the trees and saw honey **flowing**, but **no man tasted** it. For the people were **afraid** of Saul's **promise**. But **Jonathan** had not heard his father make the promise to the people. So he put the **stick** that was in his hand into the **honeycomb**. Then he put it to his mouth, and his eyes became **bright**.

1 SAMUEL 14:25–27 NLV

SPOTTY HEADLINE

FIR●T-CENT●RY BELIEVERS CELEBR●TE ●A● OF RESURRECTIO●

Hint: On the first day of the week. . .

___ ___ ___ ___ ___ ___

Q	P	T	H	G	I	R	B	P	N
H	O	N	E	Y	T	G	F	R	A
O	Z	E	F	X	T	X	W	O	H
N	M	L	V	L	R	T	T	M	T
E	K	P	K	M	O	A	N	I	A
Y	N	O	X	C	S	W	S	S	N
C	O	E	J	T	I	E	I	E	O
O	M	P	E	K	E	T	Q	N	J
M	A	D	T	R	W	N	S	J	G
B	N	K	T	D	I	A	R	F	A

BIBLE DIAMOND

N
O
I
B
K
S
L
S
E

CLUES

Sometimes friendly; sometimes romantic (Luke 22:47):

K ___ ___ ___

Covers your body (Exodus 34:29): ___ ___ ___ ___

Kingly; upright; good (Isaiah 32:8 SKJV):

___ ___ ___ ___ ___

	1	2	3	4	5
1	B	K	O	J	D
2	H	W	A	Z	N
3	F	R	Q	S	G
4	P	U	C	Y	I
5	E	L	T	M	V

Nehemiah 2:4 KJV

53-21-51-25 53-21-51 12-45-25-35 34-23-45-15 42-25-53-13 54-51, 31-13-32 22-21-23-53 15-13-34-53 53-21-13-42 54-23-12-51 32-51-33-42-51-34-53? 34-13 45 41-32-23-44-51-15 53-13 53-21-51 35-13-15 13-31 21-51-23-55-51-25.

FARMING

Across

4. "Hear ye therefore the __________ of the sower" (Matthew 13:18 KJV)

5. "Our land shall yield her __________" (Psalm 85:12 KJV)

6. "I planted the seed. __________ watered it, but it was God Who kept it growing" (1 Corinthians 3:6 NLV)

8. "The __________ truly is great, but the labourers are few" (Luke 10:2 KJV)

Down

1. "You will plant seeds in your land for six __________, and gather the grain" (Exodus 23:10 NLV)

2. "He will. . .gather His __________ into the storehouse" (Matthew 3:12 SKJV)

3. "Gather the weeds first and put them together to be __________" (Matthew 13:30 NLV)

4. "The husbandman that laboureth must be first __________ of the fruits" (2 Timothy 2:6 KJV)

7. "And God said, Behold, I have given you every herb bearing __________" (Genesis 1:29 KJV)

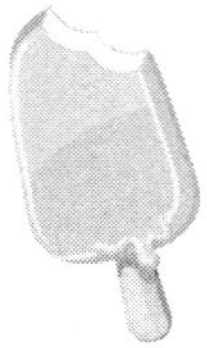

1
2
3
4
5
6
7
8

SPOTTY HEADLINE

MESS●AH C●MPARED
TO POWERFU● A●IMAL

Hint: He came from the tribe of Judah.

___ ___ ___ ___

Jesus: The Suffering Servant

For sure He took on Himself our **troubles** and **carried** our **sorrows**. Yet we **thought** of Him as being **punished** and **hurt** by God, and made to **suffer**. But He was hurt for our wrong-doing. He was **crushed** for our sins. He was punished so we would have **peace**. He was **beaten** so we would be **healed**. All of us like **sheep** have gone the **wrong way**. Each of us has turned to his own way. And the Lord has put on Him the sin of **us all**.

ISAIAH 53:4–6 NLV

SPOTTY HEADLINE

THR●E HEB●EW MEN F●●E
KI●G'S ●IERY P●NISHMENT

Hint: Don't worry—they came through okay!

___ ___ ___ ___ ___ ___ ___

K	T	N	S	O	R	R	O	W	S
P	R	E	F	F	U	S	X	D	W
U	S	T	H	E	A	L	E	D	R
N	E	A	T	W	C	I	B	D	O
I	L	E	M	H	R	A	E	T	N
S	B	B	S	R	O	H	E	U	G
H	U	D	A	H	S	U	S	P	W
E	O	C	U	U	E	A	G	N	A
D	R	R	R	R	L	E	J	H	Y
K	T	C	R	L	G	H	P	N	T

PAUL AND SILAS

ACTS 16:25 KJV

After casting a demon out of a girl, Paul and Silas were thrown into jail. Crack the code to find out what they did while behind bars.

"A certain damsel possessed with a _________ of divination met us" (16:16 KJV) 21-7-25-10-24-2

"They are telling you how to be saved from the _________ of sin" (16:17 NLV) 26-6-16-23-13-4-27-9-15-28

"The girl's owners. . .could not make _________ with her anymore" (16:19 NLV) 22-8-14-19-3

"The girl's owners. . . _________ [Paul and Silas] to the leaders" (16:19 NLV) 12-17-29-18-5-31-20

"Do not hurt yourself. We are _________ here!" (16:28 NLV) 30-1-11

29-16-12 30-2 27-25-20-15-24-18-4-28 26-29-6-1

30-14-20 21-23-11-29-13 26-17-30-3-19-12, 30-15-12

21-29-14-5 7-10-30-24-21-9-13 6-16-28-8 5-8-20: 30-14-12

2-4-31 26-17-23-21-8-14-9-17-21 4-19-29-17-12 28-4-19-22.

BIBLE DIAMOND

A
I
U
L
Q
O
N
R
U

CLUES

Birds that fell from sky (Exodus 16:13):

Q ___ ___ ___ ___

Another word for alcohol (Numbers 6:3 SKJV):

___ ___ ___ ___ ___ ___

Don't walk (2 Samuel 22:30): ___ ___ ___

Singing

Across

3. "O sing unto the LORD a ________ song: sing unto the LORD, all the earth" (Psalm 96:1 KJV)

5. "I will sing of ________ and judgment" (Psalm 101:1 KJV)

6. "In the midst of the church will I sing ________ to You" (Hebrews 2:12 SKJV)

8. "Let us. . .make a joyful noise to the ________ of our salvation" (Psalm 95:1 KJV)

9. "Make a joyful noise unto the LORD, all ye ________" (Psalm 100:1 KJV)

Down

1. Christians should sing "psalms and hymns and ________ songs" (Colossians 3:16 SKJV)

2. "Let them sing praises unto him with the timbrel and ________" (Psalm 149:3 KJV)

3. "I will sing praise to thy ________, O thou most High" (Psalm 9:2 KJV)

4. "On a ________ and an instrument of ten strings I will sing praises to You" (Psalm 144:9 SKJV)

7. "For it is ________ to sing praises to our God" (Psalm 147:1 NLV)

1
2
3
4
5
6
7
8
9

SPOTTY HEADLINE

EVE ●OOL●SHLY
EA●S J●ICY T●EAT

Hint: We still don't know what kind it was.

___ ___ ___ ___ ___

NOT OF MEN

Do you **think** I am **trying** to get the **favor** of **men**, or of God? If I were still trying to **please** men, I would not be a servant **owned** by Christ. **Christian brothers**, I want you to know the **Good News** I **preached** to you was not **made** by man. I did not receive it from man. No one **taught** it to me. I received it from Jesus Christ as He **showed** it to me.

GALATIANS 1:10–12 NLV

SCRAMBLED PERSONS

PEN THE JORDAN

Hint: First disciples to see Jesus' empty tomb

___ ___ ___ ___ ___   ___ ___ ___

___ ___ ___ ___

D	N	A	I	T	S	I	R	H	C
E	T	M	T	A	U	G	H	T	F
H	D	K	E	H	Z	D	S	O	G
C	E	N	B	N	D	R	W	N	O
A	W	I	F	D	E	N	I	P	O
E	O	H	E	H	E	Y	F	L	D
R	H	T	T	D	R	D	B	E	N
P	S	O	H	T	A	X	B	A	E
M	R	F	C	R	X	M	J	S	W
B	C	F	A	V	O	R	H	E	S

DECODER

	1	2	3	4	5
1	A	U	P	Y	K
2	D	Z	S	C	H
3	G	O	F	R	V
4	M	B	L	E	Q
5	N	T	J	W	I

Isaiah 53:6 SKJV

54-44 11-43-43 43-55-15-44 23-25-44-44-13 25-11-35-44 31-32-51-44 11-23-52-34-11-14. 54-44 25-11-35-44 52-12-34-51-44-21, 44-11-24-25 32-51-44, 52-32 25-55-23 32-54-51 54-11-14, 11-51-21 52-25-44 43-32-34-21 25-11-23 43-11-55-21 52-25-44 55-51-55-45-12-55-52-14 32-33 12-23 11-43-43 32-51 25-55-41.

The Seven Churches

Revelation 3:15 SKJV

John wrote to seven churches, each having their own failures and successes. Crack the code to find out what went wrong in the church at Laodicea.

"I will give thee a _________ of life"
(2:10 KJV) 12-17-13-24-5

"I. . .will give him a _________ stone"
(2:17 KJV) 6-26-2-16-11

"You are wretched and miserable
and poor and blind and _________ "
(3:17 SKJV) 15-18-23-20-19

"I _________ you to buy from Me
gold tried in the fire" (3:18 SKJV) 10-21-3-25-14-1-22

"Let him hear what the Spirit _________
to the churches"
(3:22 SKJV) 7-4-8-9

"2 23-5-21-6 8-13-3-17 6-21-17-23-14, 16-26-4-16 8-21-3

18-17-11 25-20-2-16-26-1-17 12-13-22-19 5-21-17 26-21-16. 2

6-2-7-26 16-26-18-16 8-13-3 24-11-17-20 12-13-22-19 21-17

26-21-16."

BAPTISM

Across

2. "I baptize with __________ those who are sorry for their sins" (Matthew 3:11 NLV)

4. "Baptizing them in the name of the __________, and of the Son, and of the Holy Ghost" (Matthew 28:19 KJV)

8. "Then they that gladly __________ his word were baptized" (Acts 2:41 KJV)

Down

1. "One Lord, one __________, one baptism" (Ephesians 4:5 KJV)

3. "Be baptized, and __________ away thy sins" (Acts 22:16 KJV)

5. "Then Peter said unto them, __________, and be baptized" (Acts 2:38 KJV)

6. "He that believeth and is baptized shall be __________" (Mark 16:16 KJV)

7. "For by one Spirit are we all baptized into one __________" (1 Corinthians 12:13 KJV)

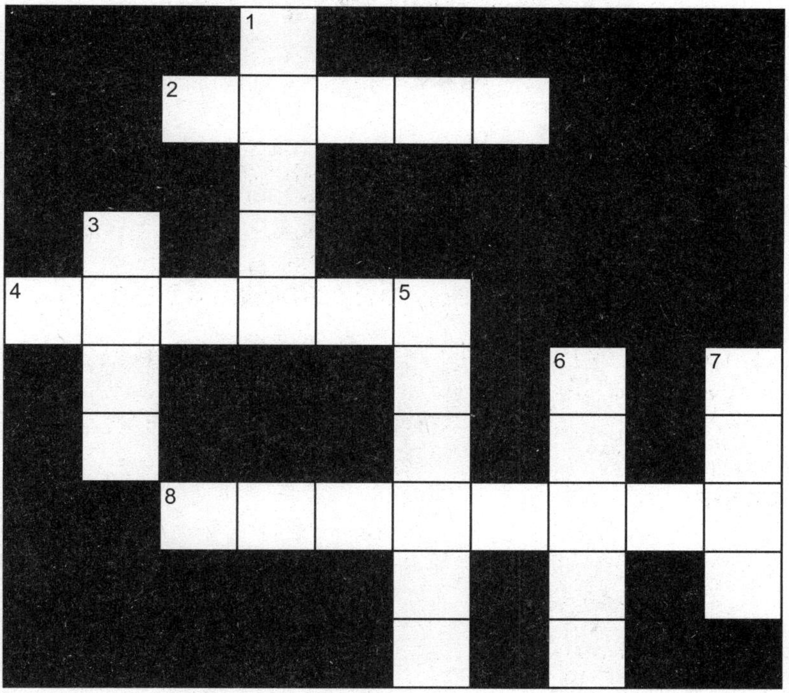
1
2
3
4
5
6
7
8

SPOTTY HEADLINE

●ELEC● ●EW CHILD●E● D●E ●ECAUSE OF PHA●A●H

Hint: It was bad to be the oldest kid in the family.

___ ___ ___ ___ ___ ___ ___ ___ ___

A MINOR SETBACK

By this time some Jews from the cities of **Antioch** and **Iconium** came. They **turned** the **minds** of the people against **Paul** and **Barnabas** and told them to throw **stones** at Paul. After they **threw** stones at him, they **dragged** him out of the city thinking he was **dead**. As the Christians gathered around Paul, he **got up** and went back into the **city**. The **next day** he went with Barnabas to **Derbe**.

ACTS 14:19–20 NLV

SPOTTY HEADLINE

M●NKIND ●OLDLY TRIES ●UI●DING TOW●R

Hint: It ended in confusion.

___ ___ ___ ___ ___

K	N	H	P	P	G	M	P	B	M
T	E	C	I	T	Y	U	A	U	M
Y	X	O	G	M	T	R	I	D	P
L	T	I	H	O	N	N	M	E	A
W	D	T	G	A	O	D	G	R	U
E	A	N	B	C	M	D	R	B	L
R	Y	A	I	B	B	I	A	E	X
H	S	E	N	O	T	S	N	E	L
T	M	D	E	G	G	A	R	D	D
T	U	R	N	E	D	L	R	K	S

DECODER

	1	2	3	4	5
1	F	W	J	X	E
2	S	G	K	D	U
3	N	O	C	P	R
4	T	B	L	H	V
5	A	Z	M	Y	I

JUDE 22 NLV

44-51-45-15 43-32-45-55-31-22 – 23-55-31-24-31-15-21-21

11-32-35 41-44-32-21-15 12-44-32 24-32-25-42-41.

A Dead Man Lives Again

JOHN 11:43 KJV

Jesus' friend had been dead for four days. . .but that didn't stop Jesus from raising him up. Crack the code to find out how He performed such an amazing feat.

"This _________ is not to death" (11:4 SKJV) — 14-4-13-23-9-12-25-10

"Are there not _________ hours in the day?" (11:9 SKJV) — 24-33-16-40-29-15

The man who died (11:14) — 3-27-34-11-35-26-18

"Let us go also so we may _________ with Jesus" (11:16 NLV) — 37-32-41

"Jews came to Martha and Mary, to _________ them" (11:19 KJV) — 28-1-21-6-38-20-39

Ran to meet Jesus when He arrived (11:20) — 8-22-30-2-7-31

"Jesus _________ " (11:35 KJV, SKJV) — 19-36-17-5

27-9-37 19-7-12-9 7-16 24-7-26-14 7-11-37 25-17-1-23-15-9,

7-41 28-35-4-36-37 33-32-39-7 22 40-38-26-37

29-1-4-13-36, 3-31-34-22-20-26-14, 13-1-21-12 6-1-30-2-7.

JESUS HEALS A BLIND MAN

Across

2. "The Jews. . .called the _________ of him that had received his sight"(John 9:18 KJV)

4. Sticky soil (John 9:6 KJV)

5. "Teacher, whose _________ made this man to be born blind?" (John 9:2 NLV)

7. "Thou art his disciple; but we are _________' disciples" (John 9:28 KJV)

8. "Go and wash in the pool of _________" (John 9:7 NLV)

Down

1. "You were born in sin. Are you trying to _________ us?" (John 9:34 NLV)

2. "They brought to the _________ him that aforetime was blind" (John 9:13 KJV)

3. "I went and washed, and I received _________ " (John 9:11 KJV)

6. "We know that _________ does not listen to sinners" (John 9:31 NLV)

1
2
3
4
5
6
7
8

SPOTTY HEADLINE

PAUL ●ENTORS AND ●NS●RUC●S ●●UNG PREAC●ER

Hint: Two books of the Bible bear his name.

___ ___ ___ ___ ___ ___ ___

Esther Saves Her People

Esther 7:10 KJV

Evil Haman had devised a scheme to kill all Jews, including Mordecai. . .but his plot backfired when Queen Esther bravely stepped in. Crack the code to find out what happened to Haman.

"The king held out to Esther the golden _________" (5:2 SKJV) 26-12-23-1-3-31-2

The king promised Esther up to half his _________ (5:6 KJV, SKJV) 17-21-15-16-25-6-5

"Let the _________ apparel be brought that the king used to wear" (6:8 SKJV) 22-29-10-13-11

Adar was the _________ month (8:12) 19-28-14-20-4-8-7

"Mordecai was great in the king's _________ " (9:4 KJV) 18-9-27-24-30

26-6 3-7-23-10 18-13-15-16-31-25 7-13-5-13-15 29-15 3-7-14

16-13-11-20-9-28-24 19-18-13-3 7-30 18-13-25

1-2-23-1-13-22-14-25 4-9-2 5-6-2-25-23-12-13-21.

3-7-14-15 28-13-26 8-7-30 17-21-15-16 ' 24 28-2-13-3-7

1-13-12-21-4-21-14-25.

	1	2	3	4	5
1	B	S	J	U	F
2	W	D	L	H	X
3	N	P	E	R	O
4	Z	I	M	C	Y
5	G	T	K	V	A

Ephesians 2:8 KJV

15-35-34 11-45 51-34-55-44-33 55-34-33 45-33

12-55-54-33-22 52-24-34-35-14-51-24 15-55-42-52-24;

55-31-22 52-24-55-52 31-35-52 35-15

45-35-14-34-12-33-23-54-33-12: 42-52 42-12 52-24-33

51-42-15-52 35-15 51-35-22.

HARD TIMES

"And write to the angel of the **church** in **Smyrna**: 'The first and the **last**, who was dead and is **alive**, says these things: I know your works, and tribulation, and **poverty** (but you are rich), and I know the **blasphemy** of those who say they are Jews and are not, but are the **synagogue** of Satan. Do not fear any of those things that you shall suffer. Behold, the devil shall **cast** some of you into **prison**, that you may be tried, and you shall have tribulation **ten days**. Be **faithful** to **death**, and I will give you a **crown** of **life**."

REVELATION 2:8–10 SKJV

SPOTTY HEADLINE

●R●VE WOMAN ●IDES IS●●ELITE SPIES

Hint: She lived on the wall of Jericho.

___ ___ ___ ___ ___

B	L	A	S	P	H	E	M	Y	Q
A	C	F	M	T	C	H	K	C	S
S	L	A	L	A	R	T	P	R	Y
Y	H	I	S	Y	P	A	O	O	N
A	C	T	V	J	T	E	V	W	A
D	R	H	B	E	W	D	E	N	G
N	U	F	N	O	S	I	R	P	O
E	H	U	C	T	T	Y	T	G	G
T	C	L	W	R	M	L	Y	K	U
L	A	S	T	S	E	F	I	L	E

Forty Days of Weakness

LUKE 4:2 NLV

Fasting in the wilderness for forty days, Jesus proved that even when His body grew weak, His spirit was stronger than ever. Crack the code to find out what He faced while in the desert.

"Command this stone that it be made _________" (4:3 KJV) 27-7-28-8-35

Jesus was brought onto a high _________ (4:5) 36-15-32-16-31-17-25-30

"All this power will I _________ thee" (4:6 KJV) 4-1-20-9

"If You will _________ me, all this will be Yours" (4:7 NLV) 21-5-29-13-2-18-23

"If thou be the Son of God, cast _________ down from hence" (4:9 KJV) 6-26-33-19-12-14-3

"He shall give his _________ charge over thee" (4:10 KJV) 34-11-10-24-37-22

2-28 21-34-19 31-9-36-23-6-12-35 27-33 31-2-24

35-28-20-25-14 3-15-7 3-5-29-6-33 35-34-33-22 8-16-35

2-9 17-31-24 11-15-6-26-25-30-10 35-32-29-18-11-4

6-2-8-6 6-1-36-28. 34-3-31-9-29 6-26-8-31 2-9 21-34-13

2-32-11-4-29-33.

DECODER

	1	2	3	4	5
1	A	S	L	P	G
2	R	E	Y	J	O
3	M	W	Z	H	K
4	I	F	T	V	U
5	N	B	X	C	D

TITUS 2:11 KJV

42-25-21 43-34-22 15-21-11-54-22 25-42 15-25-55

43-34-11-43 52-21-41-51-15-22-43-34

12-11-13-44-11-43-41-25-51 34-11-43-34 11-14-14-22-11-21-22-55

43-25 11-13-13 31-22-51.

ANSWER KEY

BIBLE DIAMOND PUZZLES

P. 7

T
E Y
R P A
O D
A

PETER
ROAD
DAY

P. 17

H
A A
J L Y
I E
F

LIFE
ELIJAH
HAY

P. 28

A
E R
N S T
I H
N

SIN
NINE
EARTH

P. 37

N
T U
R S N
I O
L

SUN
NUN
NOSTRIL

P. 47

E
I K
R B O
E R
I

BRIER
RIB
BROKE

P. 57

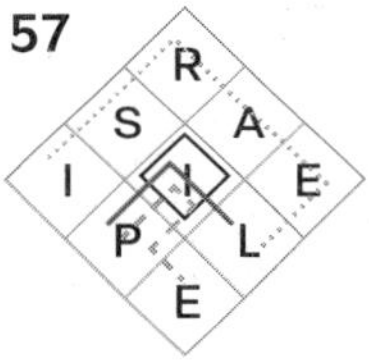
R
S A
I I E
P L
E

ISRAEL
LIP
PIPE

P. 67

V
E O
L H L
S Y
E

HOLY
YES
SHOVEL

P. 77

H
A C
O T U
B O
M

TOMB
BOAT
TOUCH

P. 87

R
E R
D C E
K T
S

CRETE
ERRED
DECKS

P. 97

Y
G P
D E T
E R
N

EGYPT
TREE
EDEN

P. 107

W
A L
E L S
K N
A

LAW
WALLS
SNAKE

P. 117

R
D O
E B W
A H
T

BOW
WORD
DEATH

P. 130

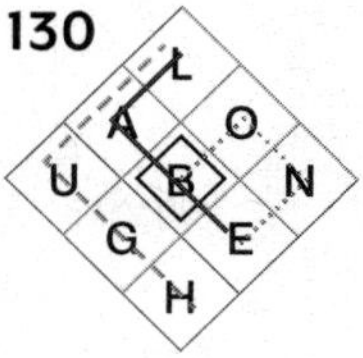
L
A O
U B N
G E
H

BONE
EBAL
LAUGH

P. 137

A
E T
N S L
O O
M

SOLOMON
NOSE
EAT

P. 150

I
O L
N E N
G O
L

EGLON
NOEL
LION

P. 160

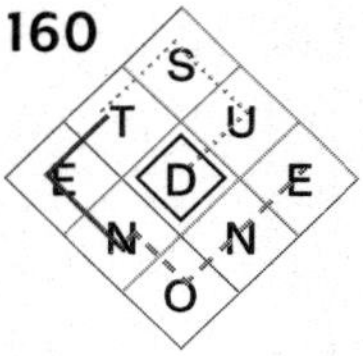
S
T U
E D E
N N
O

DUST
TEN
NONE

P. 170

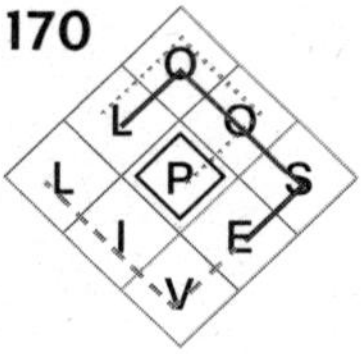
O
L O
L P S
I E
V

POOL
LOOSE
EVIL

P. 180

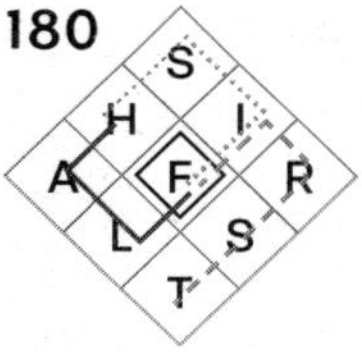
S
H I
A F R
L S
T

FISH
HALF
FIRST

P. 187

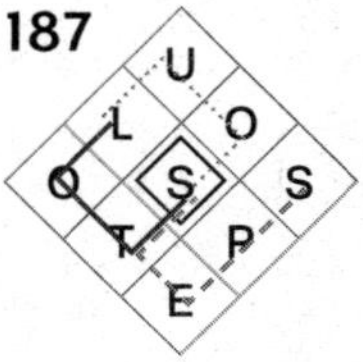
U
L O
O S S
T P
E

SOUL
LOTS
STEPS

P. 198

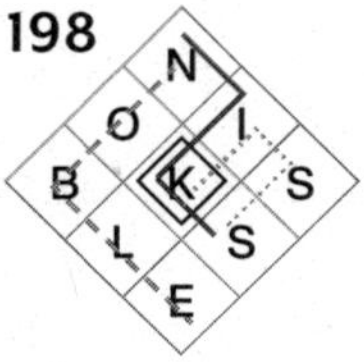
N
O I
B K S
L S
E

KISS
SKIN
NOBLE

P. 205

A
I U
L Q O
N R
U

QUAIL
LIQUOR
RUN

WORD SEARCHES

P. 9

D	S	G	N	I	H	T	R	J	L
H	E	D	O	J	K	J	C	S	I
I	T	L	B	D	Q	T	I	T	K
S	T	T	L	R	D	N	R	A	E
O	I	H	W	I	F	I	E	K	N
W	R	I	A	U	F	W	D	L	E
N	I	N	L	Z	Y	L	H	A	S
S	P	K	D	C	F	X	U	W	S
O	S	F	L	E	S	H	P	F	H
N	D	E	N	M	E	D	N	O	C

P. 15

S	E	L	P	I	C	S	I	D	L
P	S	C	A	T	T	E	R	E	D
L	L	H	O	P	E	D	S	C	L
E	S	D	R	M	N	U	H	T	A
N	B	H	N	B	D	T	E	S	B
T	D	F	E	E	F	I	P	E	O
I	M	W	V	E	S	T	H	V	R
F	W	O	W	Y	P	L	E	R	E
U	M	K	V	R	N	U	R	A	R
L	V	X	K	V	M	M	D	H	S

P. 21

T	N	D	G	N	A	S	H	E	D
A	I	R	E	Z	P	B	G	F	N
N	S	R	B	P	E	A	R	S	A
A	T	J	I	H	P	D	M	V	H
R	A	E	O	P	E	O	A	J	T
T	N	L	E	I	S	C	T	R	H
U	D	W	R	T	C	Y	A	S	G
C	I	C	D	O	H	E	L	H	I
L	N	B	R	Y	H	M	V	O	R
J	G	D	E	N	E	P	O	K	H

P. 27

A	Z	R	E	V	E	N	E	L	L
L	I	R	R	K	V	V	D	A	R
L	Y	S	R	E	E	H	I	N	E
F	O	W	S	R	T	C	H	E	M
L	R	O	Y	E	E	A	D	E	E
E	T	B	R	P	E	O	W	W	M
S	S	N	S	Z	O	N	F	T	B
H	E	I	Y	L	P	L	T	E	E
L	D	A	F	B	L	V	M	B	R
A	G	R	E	E	M	E	N	T	R

P. 33

K	C	A	B	D	L	O	H	R	G
N	O	I	S	E	D	E	E	D	N
N	Z	M	K	M	A	D	R	P	I
E	G	Y	O	R	N	A	G	D	N
T	M	T	T	U	E	K	R	F	T
S	W	H	H	H	T	W	E	N	H
I	H	T	K	N	K	H	A	H	G
L	O	C	P	J	N	W	T	X	I
F	L	V	R	E	C	I	O	V	L
R	E	P	O	W	E	R	F	U	L

P. 39

D	I	S	T	R	E	S	S	Y	W
E	L	H	H	C	N	A	R	B	D
C	S	T	S	A	L	B	Y	U	V
A	T	G	W	F	Y	D	O	K	S
L	O	N	R	M	E	L	V	H	N
P	R	E	N	E	C	B	A	M	Q
Y	M	R	N	W	F	D	L	M	M
R	N	T	Q	M	O	U	N	O	H
D	J	S	R	W	C	D	G	F	W
G	N	I	Y	F	I	R	R	E	T

P. 45

X	B	N	P	T	N	O	R	F	C
K	A	P	D	E	I	D	H	L	J
N	D	H	C	T	R	O	R	E	K
N	A	N	O	Z	N	F	L	S	L
O	N	L	B	O	G	A	U	Y	F
T	D	X	R	N	T	U	E	M	L
H	X	E	O	G	H	T	Z	M	E
O	D	M	F	I	R	E	P	A	N
L	A	V	B	L	S	E	S	O	M
Y	A	A	R	O	N	Z	V	M	G

P. 49

B	N	T	F	T	O	O	O	L	D
D	R	E	T	F	A	G	N	O	L
D	E	S	I	M	O	R	P	E	B
C	H	I	L	D	B	A	L	T	E
W	Y	R	K	S	X	B	G	H	L
J	V	L	R	K	A	H	Y	E	I
B	S	A	I	R	R	T	N	S	E
M	T	A	G	M	N	I	A	E	V
S	J	O	N	J	A	A	M	A	E
J	D	T	W	D	T	F	Z	K	Y

P. 55

K	K	Z	K	P	A	S	S	Q	D
S	D	R	O	W	K	L	L	A	E
N	P	T	G	R	O	W	X	E	N
A	L	U	N	X	N	L	R	V	E
M	L	Y	T	E	M	T	K	L	P
F	E	N	A	S	G	R	P	F	P
O	A	R	L	I	O	O	O	D	A
N	V	A	F	K	E	U	W	O	H
O	E	E	K	P	T	Z	T	J	D
S	S	L	N	E	V	A	E	H	P

P. 59

X	B	T	H	I	T	T	I	T	E
D	R	A	F	N	Z	L	K	W	D
E	R	H	C	F	N	S	G	R	M
S	A	O	C	K	E	B	I	R	U
O	E	R	H	I	S	V	X	A	L
L	Y	N	M	R	E	P	Y	E	T
A	E	E	N	T	U	R	N	F	I
T	N	T	S	T	S	A	E	B	P
E	O	S	E	T	I	V	I	H	L
E	T	I	N	A	A	N	A	C	Y

P. 65

T	C	D	E	K	O	O	L	B	N
L	N	Q	P	V	N	M	Q	T	E
W	Y	O	W	A	A	G	G	E	M
Y	J	M	R	H	Z	D	R	N	E
F	T	G	A	F	Y	R	O	T	E
F	A	R	M	H	C	O	U	D	R
J	B	C	E	A	R	L	N	O	H
A	L	A	E	W	M	M	D	O	T
J	T	M	E	E	T	R	G	R	N
R	O	A	K	T	R	E	E	S	R

P. 69

H	S	S	I	D	E	R	O	O	P
A	G	E	T	D	S	H	A	M	E
R	A	R	H	H	E	D	K	R	C
D	T	E	G	C	K	S	Y	V	F
W	H	M	I	S	I	R	I	E	Y
O	E	M	R	I	G	R	S	R	L
R	R	U	X	N	N	I	X	A	E
K	I	S	U	F	W	V	Z	X	V
E	N	H	P	U	X	Y	N	N	L
R	G	Q	S	L	E	E	P	S	N

P. 75

G	O	O	D	M	A	N	T	F	P
H	T	S	R	I	F	S	I	Y	E
D	G	R	A	P	E	S	A	H	R
Y	O	T	C	V	M	C	W	H	I
T	E	O	R	Z	S	L	N	U	S
N	O	A	L	O	I	U	I	N	H
F	H	E	U	B	E	S	E	T	E
R	R	L	A	D	O	T	I	S	D
M	G	P	N	T	W	E	L	B	P
L	J	T	H	G	I	R	P	U	N

P. 79

X	T	C	Z	S	D	D	L	Y	N
P	M	N	H	E	U	A	N	L	T
U	X	D	W	A	M	M	D	I	F
N	M	O	B	O	N	L	M	L	M
I	H	G	S	X	Z	G	Y	E	K
S	F	D	B	A	S	K	E	T	R
H	R	R	X	P	E	O	P	L	E
I	U	O	T	O	N	L	L	I	W
N	I	L	D	N	E	E	H	T	T
G	T	L	E	A	R	S	I	L	C

P. 85

D	E	D	N	A	M	M	O	C	D
V	H	I	D	E	K	R	L	R	Y
B	K	V	M	G	A	M	A	Y	D
M	R	X	X	V	H	W	R	A	C
E	Y	O	E	D	T	M	E	W	H
A	N	N	O	S	E	R	R	A	E
T	S	H	A	K	B	E	O	T	R
D	W	E	L	L	E	D	F	E	I
M	O	R	N	I	N	G	E	G	T
G	N	I	N	E	V	E	B	H	H

P. 89

K	A	E	P	S	R	D	S	C	X
E	X	V	R	P	Y	D	E	O	T
K	M	A	E	E	G	N	N	M	O
C	E	A	L	R	C	U	O	E	G
H	O	L	N	X	Y	O	B	T	E
R	A	V	F	R	N	R	Y	O	T
V	N	V	E	L	L	A	R	L	H
M	A	N	Y	R	I	N	D	I	E
L	O	R	D	P	V	R	K	F	R
P	J	O	I	N	E	X	R	E	W

P. 95

N	R	P	F	N	C	N	R	D	P
Y	S	W	E	E	C	T	O	E	M
A	E	B	P	E	S	V	S	R	A
P	M	H	U	I	L	N	E	E	J
O	A	N	R	R	B	S	H	V	O
S	J	H	Y	M	I	N	A	I	R
T	C	B	B	D	X	E	T	L	I
L	E	V	L	E	W	T	D	E	T
E	H	U	N	D	R	E	D	D	Y
S	C	R	I	P	T	U	R	E	S

P. 99

C	D	E	T	A	E	R	C	T	C
R	E	G	N	O	L	O	N	J	Q
B	F	T	S	Z	R	E	D	P	P
M	O	H	R	W	M	K	U	Z	L
L	R	I	T	I	O	D	L	I	A
L	E	N	T	I	E	R	V	X	E
E	V	G	V	T	N	E	E	J	S
G	E	S	F	N	S	I	D	R	E
N	R	I	D	H	A	N	D	M	H
A	L	L	M	Y	B	F	K	Y	T

P. 105

D	O	G	F	O	Y	R	O	L	G
L	A	M	B	R	K	D	K	Y	E
C	M	O	N	L	E	M	T	R	L
S	G	O	P	V	T	H	J	T	P
N	A	N	A	M	G	H	M	H	M
O	T	S	C	I	H	S	G	G	E
I	E	R	M	I	H	O	C	I	T
T	S	L	J	I	T	F	N	N	L
A	A	N	N	L	R	Y	F	O	H
N	D	E	K	I	N	G	S	N	R

P. 109

K	T	B	U	R	N	E	D	Q	T
S	S	E	N	I	L	D	O	G	N
D	E	V	L	O	S	S	I	D	E
S	T	N	E	M	E	L	E	Y	V
N	R	N	I	G	H	T	T	A	R
O	Y	Y	R	W	W	P	F	D	E
I	M	L	O	P	M	E	A	G	F
S	R	R	O	E	I	T	W	S	Q
E	K	D	L	H	M	K	H	X	S
S	P	T	T	T	N	T	T	N	N

P. 115

S	E	N	O	E	L	T	T	I	L
R	M	R	R	R	Q	K	T	L	K
I	S	E	K	Z	E	N	K	O	R
G	E	T	L	N	E	W	W	S	M
H	V	A	D	S	I	H	A	E	K
T	I	W	C	K	O	R	P	R	V
E	E	T	F	E	M	Q	D	U	D
O	C	K	V	R	D	P	R	K	C
U	E	E	P	R	O	P	H	E	T
S	R	D	I	S	C	I	P	L	E

P. 119

T	S	E	C	I	O	J	E	R	G
Z	Y	R	J	D	R	C	N	N	L
K	V	V	L	A	I	P	I	E	C
F	D	R	C	R	S	H	L	D	H
N	O	E	C	D	T	U	L	D	A
W	G	U	W	O	N	P	N	I	M
C	I	N	N	P	Q	E	M	H	B
T	A	B	E	R	N	A	C	L	E
S	T	R	O	N	G	M	A	N	R
B	R	I	D	E	G	R	O	O	M

P. 125

G	R	E	A	T	S	K	I	N	V
Y	S	D	E	R	O	T	S	E	R
D	T	O	M	K	W	N	N	E	X
E	N	G	O	P	M	O	H	E	N
P	A	F	R	P	C	T	U	E	W
P	V	O	E	W	A	W	V	L	K
I	R	N	N	F	A	E	Q	K	D
D	E	A	Y	S	S	Q	L	R	F
T	S	M	H	N	A	E	L	C	T
J	O	R	D	A	N	N	T	G	X

P. 129

L	O	V	E	L	I	N	E	S	S
Y	U	F	N	H	G	R	S	T	Y
L	R	G	W	R	T	R	D	W	F
E	G	W	L	U	E	A	A	I	G
R	O	P	O	H	G	F	E	S	L
U	D	Y	T	R	J	L	C	R	S
S	R	I	B	M	D	O	I	R	B
C	W	W	H	A	T	W	O	N	T
K	S	E	D	A	F	E	V	R	M
F	O	R	E	V	E	R	T	X	Z

P. 135

G	R	L	E	B	A	N	O	N	K
E	L	P	K	G	Y	R	T	B	S
S	R	M	L	K	O	M	I	R	N
U	O	K	L	A	N	A	A	F	M
O	C	N	H	E	N	D	T	C	A
H	K	L	S	Y	E	T	X	S	K
R	S	T	H	C	R	P	E	C	E
J	S	G	H	P	P	A	W	D	B
P	I	K	R	O	T	S	X	W	R
H	H	I	L	L	S	M	D	J	L

P. 139

E	L	N	E	R	D	L	I	H	C
T	H	A	T	E	N	Z	P	U	G
U	L	R	X	F	S	B	N	O	R
C	B	C	E	D	Q	J	O	O	T
E	Y	L	N	H	U	D	B	C	H
S	Z	E	E	S	T	H	D	U	E
R	S	V	T	S	G	A	T	R	E
E	C	O	X	I	S	T	F	S	V
P	Q	L	E	Y	A	R	P	E	I
Q	M	N	F	P	J	U	S	T	L

P. 145

D	E	H	C	T	I	W	E	B	N
E	F	O	R	M	E	R	L	Y	O
N	T	L	M	N	N	K	L	Z	I
O	S	T	S	I	E	Q	D	N	T
T	E	R	O	A	P	M	P	D	N
A	T	E	R	T	M	O	I	O	E
E	A	G	C	R	W	A	M	T	T
R	E	A	E	E	X	I	R	P	T
G	R	R	R	C	S	C	W	I	A
R	G	D	Y	L	E	A	S	T	A

P. 149

N	N	V	E	W	E	S	T	S	K
K	G	S	B	B	Y	W	J	H	P
M	I	L	S	K	M	Y	K	O	K
R	O	G	S	A	C	L	K	W	N
W	R	Q	K	K	P	O	Y	E	R
T	A	E	H	M	R	O	M	R	E
E	M	I	T	S	I	H	T	E	C
H	Y	P	O	C	R	I	T	E	S
R	V	M	B	H	Z	W	M	S	I
M	S	O	U	T	H	W	I	N	D

P. 155

C	M	W	A	G	O	N	R	M	M
B	R	D	D	S	E	S	R	O	H
T	O	E	E	E	L	I	S	H	A
T	T	S	K	E	M	N	O	P	U
W	S	S	L	T	M	Q	S	K	H
I	D	O	A	W	A	P	K	A	L
C	N	R	T	R	I	K	J	V	E
E	I	C	A	R	Z	I	E	R	N
Z	W	K	I	H	L	G	I	N	Z
P	U	T	N	E	W	F	Y	X	L

P. 159

L	F	I	N	G	E	R	S	C	D
P	D	Z	K	Z	W	I	T	O	P
R	E	E	S	N	L	I	G	G	L
I	G	F	L	V	O	F	N	Z	A
N	R	L	E	B	O	R	V	E	S
C	E	R	S	E	U	D	I	V	T
E	M	N	S	F	T	O	J	N	E
S	E	U	E	Z	N	O	R	B	R
V	O	C	V	M	K	W	W	T	F
H	J	E	R	U	S	A	L	E	M

P. 165

Y	L	H	S	I	L	O	O	F	W
W	M	N	R	U	T	E	R	J	O
B	L	E	S	S	E	D	N	D	R
B	M	O	W	G	F	W	R	L	S
S	F	Y	E	R	O	B	E	E	H
T	H	R	T	D	Y	N	N	S	I
N	O	A	L	W	E	A	H	O	P
T	Z	L	V	K	K	V	E	R	P
K	E	M	A	E	B	M	A	A	E
F	J	T	D	J	D	F	D	G	D

P. 169

S	D	S	W	E	J	K	A	L	R
O	F	S	E	E	G	N	E	N	E
N	L	W	D	N	S	A	P	O	H
O	W	R	I	W	N	W	S	T	C
F	T	K	E	A	W	M	U	H	A
G	Q	R	H	D	N	M	S	I	E
O	E	T	U	J	N	K	E	N	T
D	A	N	C	E	F	U	J	G	C
N	Z	N	P	I	L	I	H	P	T
B	Y	O	U	K	N	O	W	X	L

P. 175

S	D	R	C	J	O	S	E	P	H
A	E	Y	P	R	A	Y	E	D	E
D	T	Y	R	H	X	L	K	M	L
U	N	X	T	T	T	C	H	A	E
J	I	R	J	O	S	E	X	T	V
Q	O	L	W	U	A	I	P	T	E
F	P	T	O	R	S	L	N	H	N
N	P	Y	T	T	A	T	F	I	L
H	A	S	C	C	S	V	U	A	M
W	Y	N	E	S	O	H	C	S	K

P. 179

W	T	J	T	O	P	N	M	D	J
D	N	E	Q	G	L	E	M	N	S
N	E	L	C	E	N	E	B	A	N
J	P	S	N	I	H	D	M	L	O
Z	O	O	E	T	E	B	N	D	W
J	T	N	A	R	I	K	G	E	W
S	U	P	E	R	T	Q	M	T	A
T	C	V	T	J	Z	D	Q	S	T
L	O	H	S	P	O	R	D	A	E
C	M	B	R	I	N	G	S	W	R

P. 185

R	G	L	G	E	T	A	W	A	Y
G	R	G	O	L	B	P	Q	D	L
I	R	T	I	O	N	J	N	Q	T
V	B	V	S	X	K	L	I	S	A
E	E	M	O	U	N	T	A	I	N
D	Y	G	T	N	M	T	G	T	G
D	E	R	A	C	A	L	A	K	E
R	B	X	R	N	W	E	N	T	L
T	O	N	E	T	T	I	R	W	S
V	V	W	O	R	S	H	I	P	F

P. 191

H	E	A	P	S	Y	J	I	W	P
T	S	T	R	E	T	C	H	E	D
D	K	C	K	V	L	N	E	N	T
T	E	N	O	F	T	D	L	O	H
T	O	S	L	R	E	R	L	B	O
D	T	A	O	T	D	P	T	W	U
A	X	W	U	O	M	S	Q	A	S
R	H	O	L	S	L	E	W	J	A
M	H	K	S	D	N	A	B	M	N
S	M	I	G	H	T	I	L	Y	D

P. 197

Q	P	T	H	G	I	R	B	P	N
H	O	N	E	Y	T	G	F	R	A
O	Z	E	F	X	T	X	W	O	H
N	M	L	V	L	R	T	T	M	T
E	K	P	K	M	O	A	N	I	A
Y	N	O	X	C	S	W	S	S	N
C	O	E	J	T	I	E	I	E	O
O	M	P	E	K	E	T	Q	N	J
M	A	D	T	R	W	N	S	J	G
B	N	K	T	D	I	A	R	F	A

P. 203

K	T	N	S	O	R	R	O	W	S
P	R	E	F	F	U	S	X	D	W
U	S	T	H	E	A	L	E	D	R
N	E	A	T	W	C	I	B	D	O
I	L	E	M	H	R	A	E	T	N
S	B	B	S	R	O	H	E	U	G
H	U	D	A	H	S	U	S	P	W
E	O	C	U	U	E	A	G	N	A
D	R	R	R	R	L	E	J	H	Y
K	T	C	R	L	G	H	P	N	T

P. 209

D	N	A	I	T	S	I	R	H	C
E	T	M	T	A	U	G	H	T	F
H	D	K	E	H	Z	D	S	O	G
C	E	N	B	N	D	R	W	N	O
A	W	I	F	D	E	N	I	P	O
E	O	H	E	H	E	Y	F	L	D
R	H	T	T	D	R	D	B	E	N
P	S	O	H	T	A	X	B	A	E
M	R	F	C	R	X	M	J	S	W
B	C	F	A	V	O	R	H	E	S

P. 215

K	N	H	P	P	G	M	P	B	M
T	E	C	I	T	Y	U	A	U	M
Y	X	O	G	M	T	R	I	D	P
L	T	I	H	O	N	N	M	E	A
W	D	T	G	A	O	D	G	R	U
E	A	N	B	C	M	D	R	B	L
R	Y	A	I	B	B	I	A	E	X
H	S	E	N	O	T	S	N	E	L
T	M	D	E	G	G	A	R	D	D
T	U	R	N	E	D	L	R	K	S

P. 223

B	L	A	S	P	H	E	M	Y	Q
A	C	F	M	T	C	H	K	C	S
S	L	A	L	A	R	T	P	R	Y
Y	H	I	S	Y	P	A	O	O	N
A	C	T	V	J	T	E	V	W	A
D	R	H	B	E	W	D	E	N	G
N	U	F	N	O	S	I	R	P	O
E	H	U	C	T	T	Y	T	G	G
T	C	L	W	R	M	L	Y	K	U
L	A	S	T	S	E	F	I	L	E

CROSSWORDS

P. 11

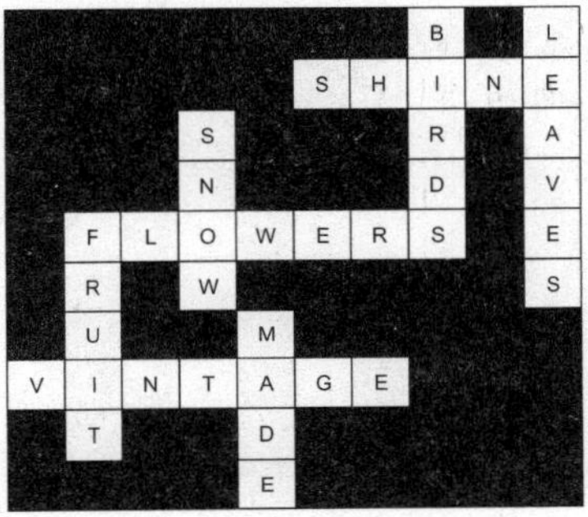

SHINE
FLOWERS
VINTAGE
BIRDS
LEAVES
SNOW
FRUIT
MADE

P. 19

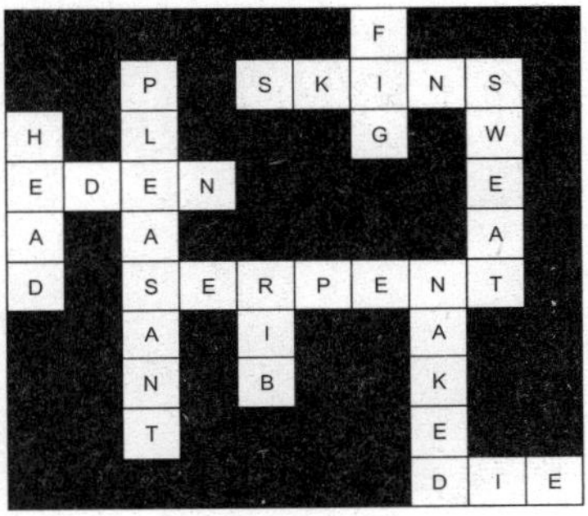

SKINS
EDEN
SERPENT
DIE
FIG
PLEASANT
HEAD
SWEAT
RIB
NAKED

P. 25

FRIEND
LAW
CHARITY
TRUTH
SINNERS
GREATEST
FEAR
WORLD
COVERS

P. 31

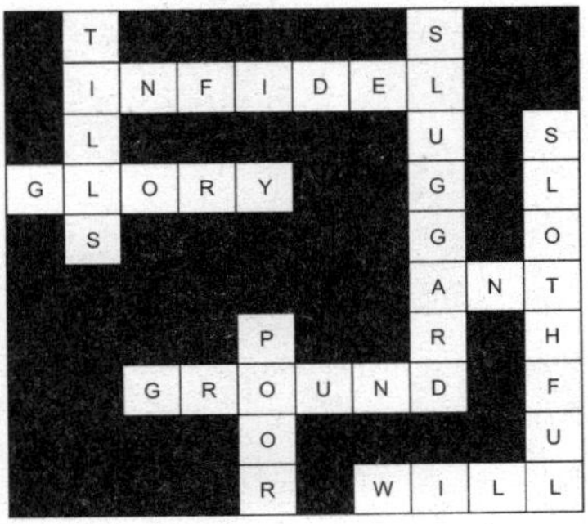

INFIDEL
GLORY
ANT
GROUND
WILL
TILLS
SLUGGARD
SLOTHFUL
POOR

P. 41

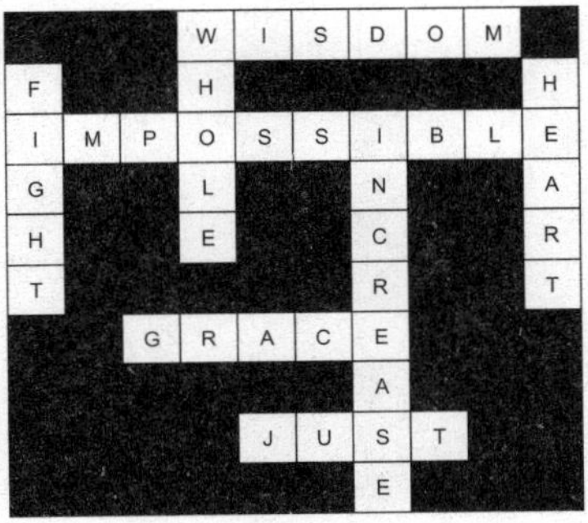

WISDOM
IMPOSSIBLE
GRACE
JUST
FIGHT
WHOLE
HEART
INCREASE

P. 53

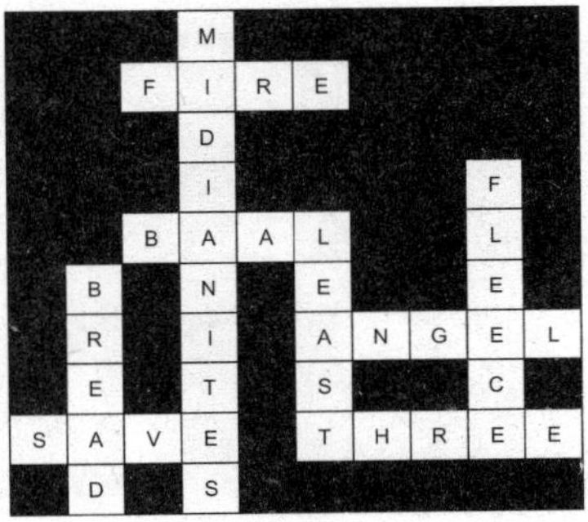

FIRE
BAAL
ANGEL
SAVE
THREE
MIDIANITES
BREAD
LEAST
FLEECE

P. 63

CRYSTAL
NARROW
ABOVE
PLACE
TREASURES
ABSENT
LAST
MANSIONS

P. 73

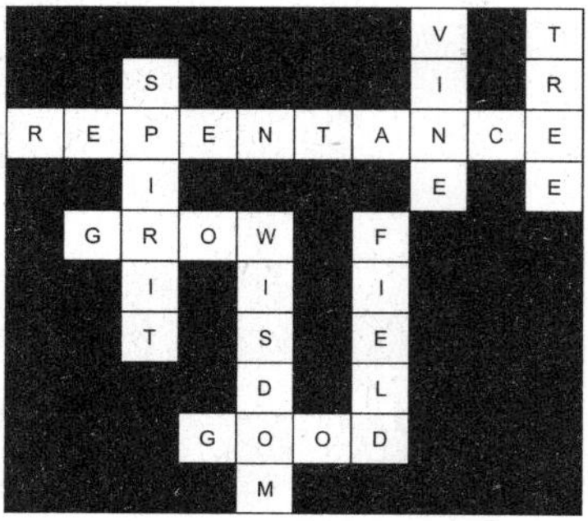
VINE
TREE
SPIRIT
REPENTANCE
GROW
WISDOM
FIELD
GOOD

P. 83

ANGEL
ARROWS
UNDER
ROAD
MOAB
SWORD
MOUTH
STICK
FOOT

P. 93

POWER
REPENT
PLEASE
MULTITUDE
MOUTH
LAW
DEATH
SHORT

P. 103

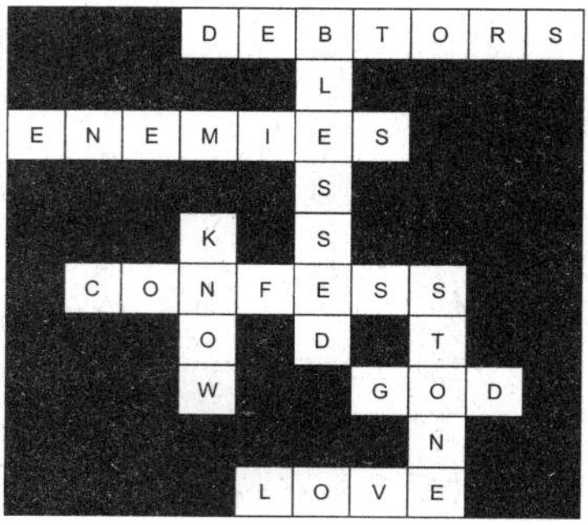
DEBTORS
BLESSED
ENEMIES
KNOW
CONFESS
STONE
GOD
LOVE

P. 113

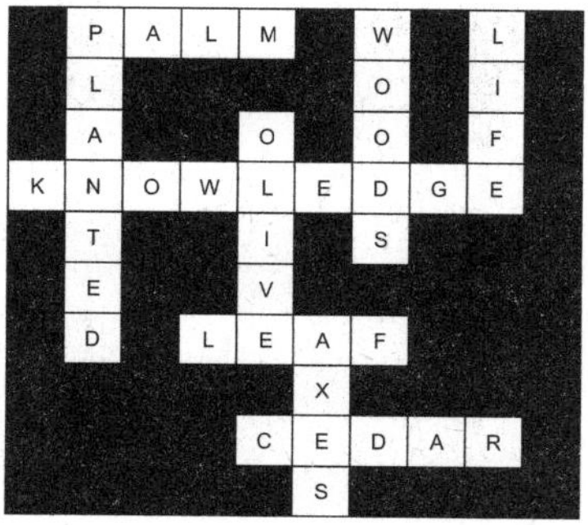
PALM
WOODS
LIFE
PLANTED
OLIVE
KNOWLEDGE
LEAF
AXES
CEDAR

P. 121

EARTH
FLOOD
PRAYED
UNJUST
SEASON
DROP
GRASS
HEAVEN

P. 127

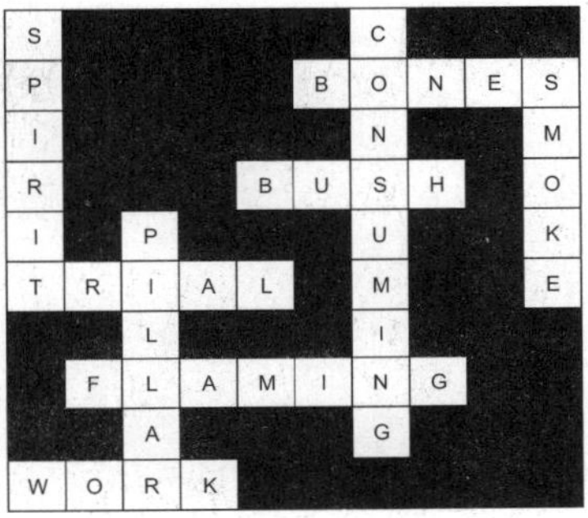
BONES
BUSH
TRIAL
FLAMING
WORK
SPIRIT
CONSUMING
SMOKE
PILLAR

P. 133

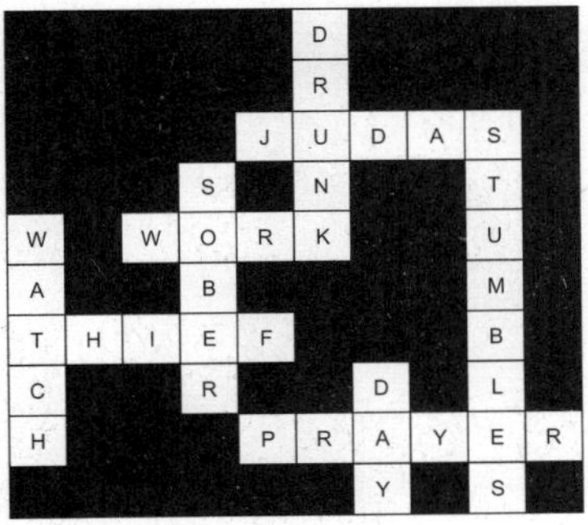
JUDAS
WORK
THIEF
PRAYER
DRUNK
STUMBLES
SOBER
WATCH
DAY

P. 143

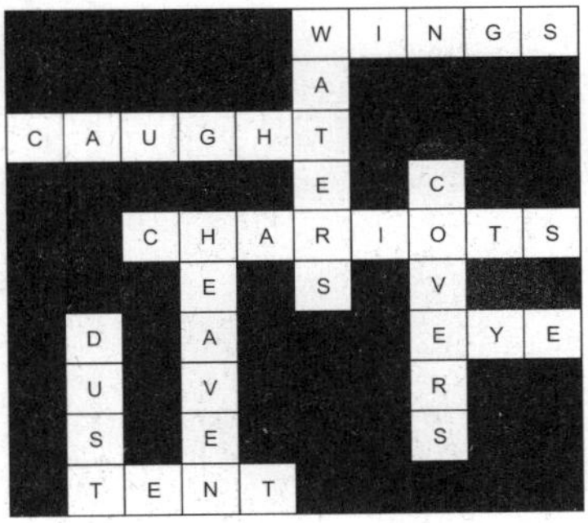
WINGS
CAUGHT
CHARIOTS
EYE
TENT
WATERS
HEAVEN
DUST
COVERS

P. 147

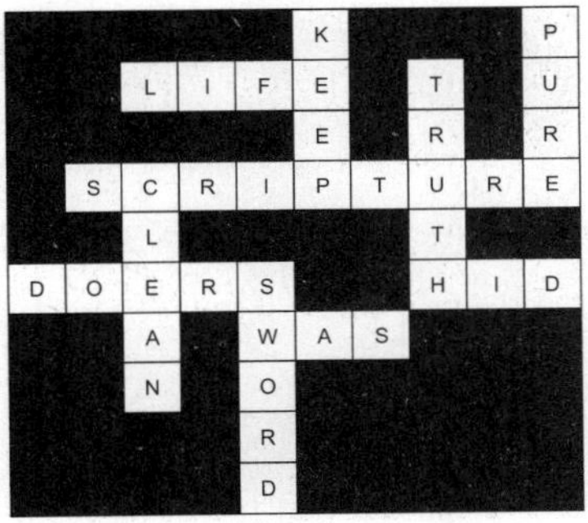
LIFE
SCRIPTURE
DOERS
HID
WAS
KEEP
PURE
TRUTH
CLEAN
SWORD

P. 153

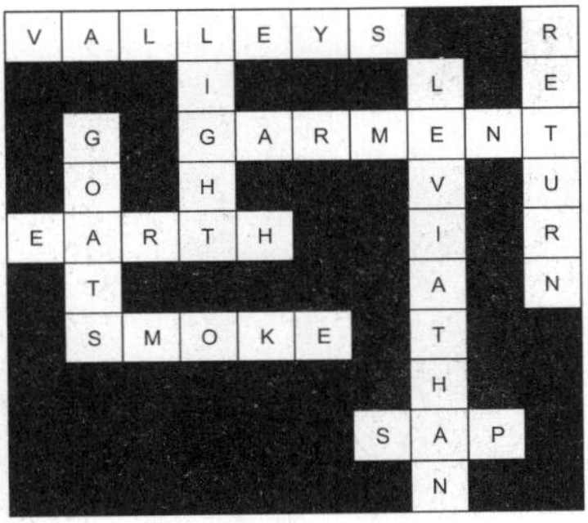
VALLEYS
GARMENT
EARTH
SMOKE
SAP
RETURN
LIGHT
GOATS
LEVIATHAN

P. 157

			C	R	Y				
	L		R				W		
	I		E				H		
	F	E	A	R		L	A	M	B
	E		T		S		L		E
			U		T		E		A
S	P	A	R	R	O	W	S		S
	L		E		R				T
	O				K				
	W								

P. 163

								C	
S	T	A	L	K	S		N	U	N
					C			R	
					A			S	
	D	E	S	T	R	O	Y	E	D
			E		L			D	
	A		V		E				
P	R	I	E	S	T	S			
	K		N			I			
						X			

P. 167

C	L	O	T	H	E	S			
						P			
			J		F	I	F	T	Y
			O			R			
W	H	I	R	L	W	I	N	D	
			D			T		O	
			A					U	
	M	A	N	T	L	E		B	
								L	
				H	O	R	S	E	S

P. 173

	P								
	E		T			R			
L	A	K	E			A			
	C		M			G		S	
	E		P	E	R	I	S	H	
			E			N		E	
	L		S			G		L	
B	O	A	T					T	
	R				W	A	V	E	S
	D							R	

P. 177

			C						
	J		I		R	E	D		A
B	O	T	T	L	E				S
	Y		Y		J				H
					O		W		E
				R	I	V	E	R	S
					C		A		
					I		K		
					N				
		L	A	U	G	H			

P. 183

	N	A	K	E	D				
				A			B		
		C	A	T	T	L	E		
		H					G		
G		E					U		
O		R		E	N	M	I	T	Y
D		U					L		
S	U	B	T	L	E		E		
		I					D	I	E
		M							

P. 189

					L				
				P	E	O	P	L	E
			S		T			A	
			H					N	
B	E	G	I	N	N	I	N	G	
R			N					U	
I		F	A	C	E			A	
C			R		A			G	
K					S			E	
			C	I	T	Y			

P. 195

		B						G	
		O		C	I	R	C	L	E
	R	U	N					A	
		N		P		P		S	
		D	R	A	G	O	N	S	
D		A		T		T			
E	A	R	T	H					
A		I		S	E	A			
D		E							
		S							

P. 201

						Y			W
	B					E			H
	U		P	A	R	A	B	L	E
	R		A			R			A
I	N	C	R	E	A	S	E		T
	E		T						
	D		A	P	O	L	L	O	S
			K						E
			E						E
	H	A	R	V	E	S	T		D

P. 207

			S						
H			P		N	E	W		
A			I		A				L
R			R		M	E	R	C	Y
P	R	A	I	S	E				R
			T			G			E
			U		R	O	C	K	
			A			O			
			L	A	N	D	S		

P. 213

			F						
		W	A	T	E	R			
			I						
	W		T						
F	A	T	H	E	R				
	S				E		S		B
	H				P		A		O
		R	E	C	E	I	V	E	D
					N		E		Y
					T		D		

P. 219

						T			
			P	A	R	E	N	T	S
			H			A			I
	C	L	A	Y		C			G
			R			H			H
		S	I	N					T
	G		S						
M	O	S	E	S					
	D		E						
			S	I	L	O	A	M	

SPOTTY HEADLINES

P. 8 MOON
P. 11 THE RED SEA
P. 14 THOMAS
P. 19 WALKS ON WATER
P. 20 GOLDEN CALF
P. 26 CANAAN
P. 31 JACOB
P. 38 RISES
P. 41 PLAGUES
P. 44 JUDGES
P. 48 JEHU
P. 54 ADAM
P. 58 TRIBES
P. 63 MIDIANITES
P. 64 MALTA
P. 73 DOVE
P. 74 HEAVEN
P. 78 BAPTIST
P. 83 SINAI
P. 88 EDEN
P. 93 JEREMIAH
P. 94 CARMEL
P. 98 SEVEN
P. 103 BETHLEHEM
P. 108 MANNA AND QUAIL

ACROSTICS

P. 12

nothing / waters / fruit / birds / male

Then God said, "Let there be light," and there was light.

P. 16

planted / mourn / gather / silence / travail / everything

To every thing there is a season, and a time to every purpose under the heaven.

P. 22

straight / flesh / behold / hollow / understanding / silver

The grass withers, the flower fades, but the word of our God shall stand forever.

P. 29

rose / apple / brought / comes / beautiful / winter / dove

The flowers appear on the earth. The time of the singing of birds has come, and the voice of the turtledove is heard in our land.

P. 34

Cursed / vengeance / mouth / freely / wrought

And all those of the land came to a wood, and there was honey on the ground.

P. 36

gather / dressed / oven / drink / holy / tomorrow / first

Even Solomon in all his glory was not arrayed like one of these.

P. 42

Enoch / righteousness / foundations / born / passover / drowned

Now faith is the substance of things hoped for, the evidence of things not seen.

P. 50

Rebekah / son / smell / dew / hunting / cry

And he said, "Your brother came with deceit and has taken away your blessing."

P. 56

came / people / thrown / against / Jesus / fear / Take / bid

Jesus said, "Come!" Peter got out of the boat and walked on the water to Jesus.

P. 61

out / Egyptians / fear / cloud / wind / horsemen

And the children of Israel went into the midst of the sea upon the dry ground.

P. 70

priest / synagogues / Damascus / city / without / vessel / suffer

And he fell to the earth and heard a voice saying to him, "Saul, Saul, why are you persecuting Me?"

P. 76

conspired / company / merchantmen / kid / wept

And they took him, and cast him into a pit: and the pit was empty, there was no water in it.

P. 86

Tarshish / wrapped / mountains / bars / thanksgiving / forty / city

Arise, go to Nineveh, that great city, and cry against it; for their wickedness is come up before me.

P. 91

wilderness / better / slept / Elijah / zealous

And Ahab told Jezebel all that Elijah had done, and withal how he had slain all the prophets with the sword.

P. 100

Galilee / Woman / hour / jars / best / good / Capernaum

And both Jesus was called, and his disciples, to the marriage.

P. 106

Blessed / earth / kingdom / body / raiment / fruits

"But seek first the kingdom of God and His righteousness, and all these things shall be added to you."

P. 116

Judah / shekels / formation / sheep / bear / living / dog

And David took the head of the Philistine, and brought it to Jerusalem; but he put his armour in his tent.

P. 123

giants / sinful / destroy / breath / clean

But Noah found grace in the eyes of the LORD.

P. 131

forty / Manoah / Judah / cords / bound / weak / Delilah

And he found a new jawbone of a donkey and stretched out his hand and took it and slew a thousand men with it.

P. 140

Mary / garden / stood / Holy / hither

Thomas said to Him, "My Lord and my God!"

P. 151

Stoics / strange / world / men / far / think

Some mocked: and others said, We will hear thee again of this matter.

P. 161

Darius / royal / name / night / servant

My God hath sent his angel, and hath shut the lions' mouths, that they have not hurt me.

P. 171

ministered / laid / for / everyone / house / knew

Now Samuel did not yet know the LORD, neither was the word of the LORD yet revealed unto him.

P. 186

wind / appeared / prophet / miracles / suffer / many

And when the day of Pentecost had fully come, they were all with one accord in one place.

P. 193

dream / child / Lebanon / fir / dwell / questions

When the queen of Sheba heard about the wisdom Solomon had from the Lord, she came to test him with hard questions.

P. 204

spirit / punishment / money / dragged / all

And at midnight Paul and Silas prayed, and sang praises unto God: and the prisoners heard them.

P. 211

crown / white / naked / counsel / says

"I know your works, that you are neither cold nor hot. I wish that you were cold or hot."

P. 217

sickness / twelve / Lazarus / die / comfort / Martha / wept

And when he thus had spoken, he cried with a loud voice, Lazarus, come forth.

P. 220

scepter / kingdom / royal / twelfth / house

So they hanged Haman on the gallows that he had prepared for Mordecai. Then was the king's wrath pacified.

P. 224

bread / mountain / give / worship / thyself / angels

He was tempted by the devil for forty days and He ate nothing during that time. After that He was hungry.

DECODERS

P. 13

"While the earth remains, seedtime and harvest, and cold and heat, and summer and winter, and day and night shall not cease."

P. 23

If the Son therefore shall make you free, ye shall be free indeed.

P. 35

The LORD on high is mightier than the noise of many waters, yea, than the mighty waves of the sea.

P. 43

And when you see the south wind blow, you say, "There will be heat." And it comes to pass.

P. 46

"They will never be hungry or thirsty again. The sun or any burning heat will not shine down on them."

P. 51

As cold waters to a thirsty soul, so is good news from a far country.

P. 60

God does not show favor to one man more than to another.

P. 66

For as in Adam all die, even so in Christ shall all be made alive.

P. 71

That at the name of Jesus every knee should bow, of things in heaven, and things in earth, and things under the earth.

P. 80

"With God are wisdom and strength. Wise words and understanding belong to Him."

P. 81

Blessed are the meek: for they shall inherit the earth.

P. 90

Honour thy father and mother; which is the first commandment with promise.

P. 96

For yourselves know perfectly that the day of the Lord so cometh as a thief in the night.

P. 101

He is the image of the invisible God, the firstborn of every creature.

P. 110

He that overcometh shall inherit all things; and I will be his God, and he shall be my son.

P. 111

In the beginning God created the heaven and the earth.

P. 122

My Christian brothers, you should be happy when you have all kinds of tests.

P. 136

Those who do not love do not know God because God is love.

P. 141

Blessed be the kingdom of our father David, that cometh in the name of the Lord: Hosanna in the highest.

P. 181

And he said to them, "I am a Hebrew, and I fear the LORD, the God of heaven, who has made the sea and the dry land."

P. 192

For every house is builded by some man; but he that built all things is God.

P. 199

Then the king said unto me, For what dost thou make request? So I prayed to the God of heaven.

P. 210

We all like sheep have gone astray. We have turned, each one, to his own way, and the LORD has laid the iniquity of us all on Him.

P. 216

Have loving-kindness for those who doubt.

P. 221

For by grace are ye saved through faith; and that not of yourselves: it is the gift of God.

P. 225

For the grace of God that bringeth salvation hath appeared to all men.

SCRAMBLES

P. 25 SEVENTH DAY
P. 32 PASSOVER LAMB
P. 53 NEW JERUSALEM
P. 68 A HUGE FISH
P. 84 KING SOLOMON
P. 104 GO TO NINEVEH
P. 121 WEDDING IN CANA
P. 143 NEW TESTAMENT
P. 154 ROSE AGAIN
P. 173 SONS OF THUNDER
P. 190 FIRMAMENT
P. 208 PETER AND JOHN